D1435954

ISLAND OF
SHADOW

The Long Grey Road to Disting (1915)
Grace Henry (1863–1953)

ISLAND OF SHADOW

IRISH POETRY ACROSS THE CENTURIES

WITH PAINTINGS BY CELEBRATED IRISH ARTISTS
SELECTED AND INTRODUCED BY BRIAN LALOR

Published in Ireland by
Gill & Macmillan
Hume Avenue, Park West, Dublin 12
with associated companies throughout the world
www.gillmacmillan.ie

Introduction © Brian Lalor 2011
ISBN 978 0 7171 5061 8

Concept and design © Bookcraft Ltd 2011   www.bookcraft.co.uk
Project managed by John Button
Designed by Lucy Guenot
Editorial and rights management by Julie Laws

Set in 12 on 19 point Plantin.

Every effort has been made to ensure the accuracy of the information presented in this book, and every reasonable effort has been
made to trace copyright holders.
The publishers will not assume liability for damages caused by inaccuracies in the data, or for any copyright inadvertently breached,
and make no warranty whatsoever expressed or implied.
The publishers welcome comments and corrections from readers, which will be incorporated in future editions.

A CIP catalogue record for this book is available from the British Library.

5   4   3   2   1

Printed in Malaysia for Imago

Contents

INTRODUCTION

BRIAN LALOR

Two languages, Irish and English, compete for the soul of Irish poetry, and their influences are so intermingled that it would be difficult, following many centuries of cross-fertilisation, to separate them. The reader will notice that some poems, both ancient and modern, are translations from Irish and some also from Latin. These texts are variously described as 'translations' or 'versions' of the originals. The different terms reflect a continuing process by which Irish writers of successive generations have sought to bring into the language of the present the literature of the past. Douglas Hyde, Frank O'Connor, Lady Gregory, Thomas Kinsella and many others have been so successful in doing this that particular translations, such as O'Connor's 'Kilcash' or Kinsella's 'Táin Bó Cúailnge' have acquired an authority within the language of their translator's own time, where the translator's poetic voice becomes for generations the accepted mouthpiece of the earlier writers. The influence of translators is sufficiently central for W.B. Yeats to fashion significant phrases in his own work from versions by O'Connor. However, versions of specific poems by different writers vary widely as the translator copes with making modern the archaic forms and concerns of other ages. The difficulty encountered by Irish writers whose mother tongue is English, in fully engaging with the language of their ancestors, finds its apogee in Michael Hartnett's 'A Farewell to English' in which, although then celebrated for his poetry in English, he announced his decision in 1975, at the age of 34, to abandon that language in favour of writing solely in Irish:

> I have made my choice
> and leave with little weeping:
> I have come with meagre voice
> to court the language of my people.

Other poets, such as Nuala Ní Dhomhnaill or Biddy Jenkinson, write solely in Irish, their poems reaching an English-speaking audience through versions by bilingual fellow-poets.

Irish painting, unlike that of most European countries, suffered a disconnect in the centuries of turmoil that followed from the twelfth-century Anglo-Norman invasion and, while a healthy and surviving sculptural tradition developed, manuscript, easel and mural painting failed to thrive. Climatic conditions, war and neglect ensured that little painting survived beyond vague traces of a vanished art. It wasn't until the seventeenth century that Irish easel-painting experienced widespread activity and the works accompanying the poems date from the eighteenth century to the present. These works show a continuing love of landscape, nature and human character, carried over from the realm of the verbal into pictorial representation. Visiting foreign artists such as Francis Wheatley and native artists like Hugh Douglas Hamilton were a dominant force during the seventeenth and eighteenth centuries while the indigenous painting tradition was beginning to find its pictorial voice. It wasn't until the late nineteenth century that what may be described as an Irish school developed, but once it had done so, it occupied what had been a vacuum and exerted an enormous influence on subsequent Irish art, right into the present. This new perception paralleled in many ways the concerns of literature, and its artists created what came to be accepted as a valid visual interpretation of Irish life. The paintings here assembled do not so much illustrate the accompanying texts as reflect some element of mood, incident, time or texture, paralleling the words thematically or conceptually, unhampered by the demand to belong to any particular era. The collective brilliance of the artists included express something of the look, the humour and the personality of both the land and the people, not only in the nineteenth century but over a much more extensive time-frame. The artists range from the most well-known names of the Irish art world to lesser figures, but all are distinguished by their serious engagement with representing and responding to the Irish emotional, intellectual and historic experience.

The earliest Irish literature, from both Latin and Irish, speaks in a voice that is alternately both humane and barbaric, stretching from the muted tones of the monastic scribes to the harsh violence and passion of the great Iron Age tribal epics. This world can be seen as distant from, or very close to, the society of the twenty-first century, and suggests a strong theme of continuity in this island people, of common preoccupations and values that stretch over a period of fifteen hundred years and embrace peoples of diverse ethnic origins. Beginning with the early Indo-European and Celtic tribes from the European mainland, and followed by Vikings, Anglo Normans, Welsh, English, Scots, Huguenots and Palatines, conquerors and settlers, all came as interlopers and ultimately were absorbed into the body politic, trailing strands of their origins in belief, behaviour and language that eventually became enmeshed in the wider consciousness of the island. Is it fancy to imagine that a voice from the remote past can speak to the reader of today? In the eleventh century Bishop Patrick writes a warm letter to his friend Bishop Wulfstan who is overseas, while in the fourteenth, Gerald Fitzgerald, Earl of Desmond, proud of the fact that he enjoyed the company of women, derides those who fail to share his enthusiasm:

Sweetly speaking, witty, clear,
Tribe most lovely to my mind,
Blame of such I hate to hear.
Speak not ill of womankind.

In the earlier centuries of monasticism, one scribe complains that his hand is weary from writing and another converses with his cat; commonplace concerns that link us across the ages. The capacity of poetry to convey the thoughts and emotions of previous generations into the present is attested to by a remarkable yet ever-changing continuity. Here, in one hundred poems from a millennium and a half, a lifeline struggles and stumbles through the prickly hawthorn hedge of Irish history with the repeated appearance of stirring and engaging work from all periods, where the complex passage of Ireland's turbulent history and life of its people is mirrored in the words of the poets. The oral tradition maintained the legends and poetry of the society since the earliest times until they were eventually transcribed in the medieval period by monastic scribes. The monks occasionally inserted Christian interpolations but generally respected the mythic quality of the narratives. But for the interest of the monastic scribes nothing would now be known of these tales of heroism and passion. While named authors do surface in early Irish literature, the vast majority of what has survived remains the work of anonymous authors.

Ireland's tribal society and geographic location on the periphery of Western Europe ensured that Renaissance ideas came very late, and the culture did not produce, in either Irish or English, a sustained humanist literature such as Geoffrey Chaucer's *The Canterbury Tales*. It was not until the late seventeenth or early eighteenth century that Irish poets merged into the European mainstream of contemporary style. The ordered, sonorous and confident world of Jonathan Swift, poet and critic of the Georgian

establishment, is one of barbed wit and classical allusions. This establishment verse is in stark contrast to the agonised lamenting of Dáibhí Ó Bruadair, whose aristocratic Gaelic society had been dispossessed by wars and religious discrimination. Swift vents his spleen on the corruptions of the age, Ó Bruadair on the indifference of a fate that has brought his proud accomplishments so low, his bardic skill and learning no longer esteemed:

Since a man is respected more
for his suit than his talents
I regret what I've spent on my art,
that I haven't it now in clothes.

Other voices from the eighteenth century, equally those of the vanished Gaelic order and that of the new ascendancy – Oliver Goldsmith, Aogán Ó Rathaille (Egan O'Rahilly), Eibhlín Dhubh Ní Chonaill and the authors of anonymous ballads – celebrate a society in turmoil with a riotous assembly of characters presented with cinematic vividness. Their word-pictures conjure up the rollicking world of gentry and peasantry, of crime and punishment:

Beauing, belling, dancing, drinking,
Breaking windows, cursing, sinking,

It is here in the eighteenth century that the high literature of the court and the demotic words of the street collide with often delightful consequences and give to Irish literature a lengthy period in which the broadside political street ballads, the popular songs and the poetry of major writers merged.

A significant product of the eighteenth century was an emerging interest in early Irish pre-Christian sagas which introduced into Irish writing a wide cast of characters who subsequently became, like the heroes of Greek and Latin literature to a classically-educated society, essential metaphors in the poet's literary arsenal. Paralleling the social confidence of the Enlightenment age, an alternate voice appears in Eibhlín Dhubh Ní Chonaill's long poem, the lament for her murdered husband, which is not only one of the greatest love poems in European literature but also amongst the most passionate literary utterances of the still vigorous Irish-speaking society. The 'Lament for Art O'Leary' forms a bridge between the oral tradition and conventional poetic compositions in being of ambiguous authorship, partly the work of the bereaved and partly a product of her society:

> My love forever!
> The day I first saw you
> At the end of the market-house,
> My eye observed you,
> My heart approved you,
> I fled from my father with you,
> Far from my home with you.

Irish poetry during the nineteenth century is dominated by political ballads celebrating the heroes and events of the centuries of conquest and persecution. Rebellions against English rule during the late eighteenth century produced a literature of poetry and ballad commemorating the dead of earlier conflicts. James Clarence Mangan, more than any of his contemporaries, emphasises the dual-language burden of Irish culture and the sense of loss regarding the Irish language in that he attempted to present translations from Irish and other languages, although he only spoke English. In Mangan's poetry can be found a primary influence of W.B. Yeats.

The late nineteenth century brings the strivings towards identity from the previous two hundred years together and the poetry of the Celtic revival is the result, with W.B. Yeats as its most significant voice. Yeats managed the difficult task of creating profoundly beautiful and meaningful poetry out of the legends and literature of the Celtic past as well as from the politics of his own time and the emotional struggles of his private life. His work became, from the 1890s to the 1930s, the dominant voice of Irish poetry and an influence which other poets found difficult to avoid. He made art out of conflict in a manner achieved by no previous Irish writer, as though the work of James Clarence Mangan, Thomas Davis, John Kells Ingram and their generation had to wait for the arrival of a supreme craftsman to put into poetry sentiments that had been attempting for generations to find a true voice. Yeats remains the Irish national poet, his work a chronicle of the emergence of modern Ireland.

Irish poetry post Yeats needed to take a sideways step in order to move away from the magisterial voice of Yeats and the Celtic Revival. It was from the realm of the emotionally dispossessed, the poor farmer, that the next major poetic direction came, in the work of Patrick Kavanagh, a voice as angry as that of Ó Bruadair, and as similarly an outsider to the literary establishment of his time. With the exception of

Francis Ledwidge, Kavanagh was unique in representing the authentic voice of rural Ireland, rather than the more commonplace idiom of that voice being interpreted by more sophisticated urban writers such as J.M. Synge, Padraic Colum or Seumas O'Sullivan, who wrote of rural themes but from the perspective of an educated elite. In 'The Great Hunger', Kavanagh uses the phrase by which the Great Famine of the 1840s was known to write about other forms of deprivation, as he railed with all the savage invective of Jonathan Swift against the spiritual poverty of the rural population of a post-colonial Ireland, denouncing equally the failings of church, state and people. Kavanagh's is one of the great independent voices in modern Irish writing.

Another, less considered because he made his career in England, is Louis MacNeice, one of many conflicted poets from Northern Ireland that include John Hewitt and Robert Greacen, all of whom struggled with the narrow definitions of Irishness prevailing in Irish writing following the partition of the island in the 1920s. MacNeice and fellow northerners felt themselves excluded from the body of Irishness, as did Kavanagh, but differently, since the north–south rift was sectarian rather than one of social class. In Hewitt's words:

> So I, because of all the buried men
> in Ulster clay, because of rock and glen
> and mist and cloud and quality of air
> as native in my thought as any here.

The combined critical voice of the northern writers introduces a necessary antidote to the more romantic and rurally focused concerns of their southern fellow poets. Austin Clarke, Kavanagh's contemporary, adopted a more austere view of poetry that ranged from the Gaelic mythological tradition to contemporary social criticism.

A pre-Raphaelite or Orientalist fancy accompanied the poetry of Yeats' period. Here J.M. Synge, Lord Dunsany, F.R. Higgins and others evoke sources of inspiration derived neither from Gaelic nor Classical literature but from Biblical and Eastern romanticism, the fascination of an imagined life in exotic climes. However, there is an underlying melancholy and latent violence to such compositions where Synge numbered the queens of the past or Higgins contemplated the Biblical Jezabel:

> King Jehu he drove to her,
> She tipped him a fancy beck;
> But he from his knacky side-car spoke,

'Who'll break that dewlapped neck?'
And so she was thrown from the window;
Like Lucifer she fell
Beneath the feet of the horses and they beat
The light out of Jezebel.

The lyric tradition of nature and love poetry to be found so prominently in the earliest survivals from the Iron Age and Early Medieval periods has its resonances in many singular pieces from recent writers – Michael Hartnett, Seamus Heaney and Macdara Woods – where the simplest of imagery is used to great poetic effect and where the most tenuous of description conjures separate imagined worlds.

A return also to the use of Classical allusion can be found in Eiléan Ní Chuilleanáin's or Michael Longley's work, where the references are not to the easily recognised figures of Irish myth, but to the great literature that sustained Western European literature for two thousand years. 'Savage indignation' in the tradition of Jonathan Swift and Patrick Kavanagh again makes its appearance in the surreal and satiric work of Paul Durcan, who exercises a fertile imagination in tilting at the absurdities of the age:

After a Spring meeting in their nineteenth-century fastness at
  Maynooth
The Irish Hierarchy has issued a total ban on the practice of
  colour photography.

Injustice, inequality, bigotry, the failings of society, sexuality, all have, in the late twentieth and early twenty-first centuries, occupied the attention of many Irish poets who, in previous ages, were more constrained by literary conventions. The bleak savagery of Patrick Galvin's 'The Madwoman of Cork' or James Simmons' 'Claudy', which deal with mental instability and the carnage caused by terrorism, give voice to the previously unspeakable trials of life.

The poetic voice of a society over a millennium and a half represents not only the areas of language, belief, politics, myth and fancy but must also carry some sense of the spirit of the people over such a lengthy period. In the twelfth century, the Anglo-Welsh chronicler Giraldus Cambrencis, who accompanied the Norman invasion of Ireland and was himself no admirer of the Irish, remarked on the Irish people's 'ornate rhythms and profusely intricate polyphony'. Despite bridging an internal emigration from the Irish language to English which took place over a three-hundred year time-span, some essences remain: lyric form, love of paradox and love of nature. In a deft twist of traditional imagery, Leslie Daiken alerts the reader to the fact that all may not be well in the mythic isle:

Island of Shadow
Silk of the Kine
Will Sickle and Hammer
Ever be thine?

The Sonnet
William Mulready (1786–1863)

THE MYSTERY

Anon

I am the wind which breathes upon the sea,

I am the wave of the ocean,

I am the murmur of the billows,

I am the ox of the seven combats,

I am the vulture upon the rocks,

I am a beam of the sun,

I am the fairest of plants,

I am a wild boar in valour,

I am a salmon in the water,

I am a lake in the plain,

I am a word of science,

I am the point of the lance of battle,

I am the God who created in the head the fire.

Who is it that throws light into the meeting on the mountain?

Who announces the ages of the moon?

Who teaches the place where couches the sun?

(If not I)

Translated by Douglas Hyde

Knockalough, Summer (1977)
Brian Bourke (1936–)

EXILE OF THE SONS OF UISLIU *from* TÁIN BÓ CÚAILNGE
Anon

Exile of the Sons of Uisliu is a prose tale, in Old Irish, of the Ulster cycle, of which the great *Táin Bó Cúailnge* – the invasion of Ulster by the armies of Connacht – is the central epic. Deirdre, the heroine of the tale, is also one of the causes of the *Táin*. In the later elaborate versions of the tale she becomes the romantic Deirdre of the Sorrows. Thomas Kinsella, in his translation of *The Táin*, uses the earliest version, which survives in a spare and forceful prose, intensifying to verse as the narrative requires. This is the opening of the tale.

What caused the exile of the sons of Uisliu? It is soon told. The men of Ulster were drinking in the house of Conchobor's storyteller, Fedlimid mac Daill. Fedlimid's wife was overseeing everything and looking after them all. She was full with child. Meat and drink were passed round, and a drunken uproar shook the place. When they were ready to sleep the woman went to her bed. As she crossed the floor of the house the child screamed in her womb and was heard all over the enclosure. At that scream everyone in the house started up, ready to kill. Sencha mac Ailella said: 'No one move! Bring the woman here. We'll see what caused this noise.' So the woman was brought before them. Her husband Fedlimid said:

'Woman,
what was that fierce shuddering sound
furious in your troubled womb?
The weird uproar at your waist
hurts the ears of all who hear it.
My heart trembles at some great terror
or some cruel injury.'

She turned distracted to the seer Cathbad:

'Fair-faced Cathbad, hear me
— prince, pure, precious crown,
grown huge in druid spells.
I can't find the fair words
that would shed the light of knowledge
for my husband Fedlimid,
even though it was the hollow
of my own womb that howled.
No woman knows what her womb bears.'

Then Cathbad said:

'A woman with twisted yellow tresses,
green-irised eyes of great beauty
and cheeks flushed like the foxglove
howled in the hollow of your womb.
I say that whiter than the snow
is the white treasure of her teeth;
Parthian-red, her lip's lustre.
Ulster's chariot-warriors
will deal many a blow for her.
There howled in your troubled womb
a tall, lovely, long-haired woman.

Mother and Child
Evie Hone (1894–1955)

Heroes will contend for her,
high kings beseech on her account;
then, west of Conchobor's kingdom
a heavy harvest of fighting men.
High queens will ache with envy
to see those lips of Parthian-red
opening on her pearly teeth,
and see her pure perfect body.'

Cathbad placed his hand on the woman's belly and the baby wriggled under it. 'Yes,' he said, 'there is a girl there. Derdriu shall be her name. She will bring evil.' Then the daughter was born and Cathbad said:

'Much damage, Derdriu, will follow
your high fame and fair visage :
Ulster in your time tormented,
demure daughter of Fedlimid.

And later, too, jealousy
will dog you, woman like a flame,
and later still — listen well —
the three sons of Uisliu exiled.

Then again, in your lifetime,
a bitter blow struck in Emain.
Remorse later for that ruin
wrought by the great son of Roech;

Fergus exiled out of Ulster
through your fault, fatal woman,
and the much-wept deadly wound
of Fiachna, Conchobor's son.

Your fault also, fatal woman,
Gerrce felled, Illadan's son,
and a crime that no less cries out,
the son of Durthacht, Eogan, struck.

Harsh, hideous deeds done
in anger at Ulster's high king,
and little graves everywhere
— a famous tale, Derdriu.'

'Kill the child!' the warriors said. 'No,' Conchobor said. 'The girl will be taken away tomorrow. I'll have her reared for me. This woman I'll keep to myself.' The men of Ulster didn't dare speak against him.

Translated by Thomas Kinsella

DONAL OGE: GRIEF OF A GIRL'S HEART

Anon

O Donal Oge, if you go across the sea,

Bring myself with you and do not forget it;

And you will have a sweetheart for fair days and market days,

And the daughter of the King of Greece beside you at night.

It is late last night the dog was speaking of you;

The snipe was speaking of you in her deep marsh.

It is you are the lonely bird through the woods;

And that you may be without a mate until you find me.

You promised me, and you said a lie to me,

That you would be before me where the sheep are flocked;

I gave a whistle and three hundred cries to you,

And I found nothing there but a bleating lamb.

You promised me a thing that was hard for you,

A ship of gold under a silver mast;

Twelve towns with a market in all of them,

And a fine white court by the side of the sea.

You promised me a thing that is not possible,

That you would give me gloves of the skin of a fish;

That you would give me shoes of the skin of a bird;

And a suit of the dearest silk in Ireland.

Awaiting the Sailor's Return
David Woodlock (1842–1929)

Going to the Market
Francis Wheatley (1747–1801)

O Donal Oge, it is I would be better to you
Than a high, proud, spendthrift lady:
I would milk the cow; I would bring help to you;
And if you were hard pressed, I would strike a blow for you.

O, ochone, and it's not with hunger
Or with wanting food, or drink, or sleep,
That I am growing thin, and my life is shortened;
But it is the love of a young man has withered me away.

It is early in the morning that I saw him coming,
Going along the road on the back of a horse;
He did not come to me; he made nothing of me;
And it is on my way home that I cried my fill.

When I go by myself to the Well of Loneliness,
I sit down and I go through my trouble;
When I see the world and do not see my boy,
He that has an amber shade in his hair.

It was on that Sunday I gave my love to you;
The Sunday that is last before Easter Sunday.
And myself on my knees reading the Passion;
And my two eyes giving love to you for ever.

O, aya! my mother, give myself to him;

And give him all that you have in the world;

Get out yourself to ask for alms,

And do not come back and forward looking for me.

My mother said to me not to be talking with you, to-day,

Or to-morrow, or on Sunday;

It was a bad time she took for telling me that;

It was shutting the door after the house was robbed.

My heart is as black as the blackness of the sloe,

Or as the black coal that is on the smith's forge;

Or as the sole of a shoe left in white halls;

It was you put that darkness over my life.

You have taken the east from me; you have taken the west from me,

You have taken what is before me and what is behind me;

You have taken the moon, you have taken the sun from me,

And my fear is great that you have taken God from me!

Translated by Lady Augusta Gregory

PANGUR BÁN

Anon

I and Pangur Bán, my cat,
'Tis a like task we are at;
Hunting mice is his delight,
Hunting words I sit all night.

Better far than praise of men
'Tis to sit with book and pen;
Pangur bears me no ill will,
He too plies his simple skill.

'Tis a merry thing to see
At our tasks how glad are we,
When at home we sit and find
Entertainment to our mind.

Oftentimes a mouse will stray
In the hero Pangur's way;
Oftentimes my keen thought set
Takes a meaning in its net.

'Gainst the wall he sets his eye
Full and fierce and sharp and sly;
'Gainst the wall of knowledge I
All my little wisdom try.

When a mouse darts from its den,
O how glad is Pangur then!
O what gladness do I prove
When I solve the doubts I love!

So in peace our tasks we ply,
Pangur Bán, my cat and I;
In our hearts we find our bliss,
I have mine and he has his.

Practice every day has made
Pangur perfect in his trade;
I get wisdom day and night
Turning darkness into light.

Translated by Robin Flower

Book of Kells fol. 48r, Cat and Mouse
Anonymous Celtic scribe (*c.*800)

THE NUN OF BEARE

Anon

Ebb to me, unlike the sea's; old age makes me yellow.

Though I may grieve at it, happily does its tide return.

I am the Nun of Béarra Baoi.

I used to wear a shift that was always new.

Today I have become so thin that I would not wear out even an old shift.

It is riches you love, not people; when we were alive, it was people we loved.

Dear were the people whose plains we ride about;

Well did we fare among them, and they made little boast of it thereafter.

Today they ask nicely, and it is not much they will pay back;

Although they give little, they let us off a lot.

Swift chariots and horses that won the prize, once I had plenty of them —

God rest the king who gave them.

My body fearfully seeks its way to the house of judgement;

When the Son of God thinks it time, let Him come to take his loans.

Bony and thin are my hands; dear was the trade they practised,

They would be around splendid kings.

Bony and thin are my hands;

I swear they are not worth raising above pretty boys.

The girls are joyous when May approaches.

Sorrow is more fitting for me; I am not only sad, but an old woman.

I pour out no good sweet ale, no wethers are killed for my wedding;

My hair is grey and scanty, it is no loss to have a miserable veil over it.

I do not care if there is a white veil on my head;

I had coverings of every colour on my head when I drank good ale.

I do not envy anything old except Femen;

While I have gone through old age Femen's crown is still yellow.

The King's Stone in Femen, Rónán's fort in Bregon,

Storms have long since reached them, but their cheeks are not old and withered.

The wave of the great sea is noisy, winter has stirred it up;

I do not expect nobleman or slave's son to visit me today.

It is many a day since I sailed on the sea of youth;

Many years of my beauty have departed because wantonness has spent itself.

It is many a day since I have been warm;

I have to take my shawl even in sunlight, for old age sets on one like me.

Youth's summer that I knew I have spent with its autumn,

Wintry age that smothers everyone has begun to approach me.

I wasted my youth to begin with, and I am glad I decided it thus;

Even if I had not been venturesome, the cloak would now be new no longer.

Beautiful is the distant cloak which the King has thrown over the hillside;

The fuller who has covered its bareness is a craftsman.

God help me! I am a poor wretch; each bright eye has decayed.

After feasting by bright candles, I am in the darkness of a wooden church.

I have had my time with kings, drinking mead and wine;

Today I drink whey and water among withered old women.

Let my ale-feast be a cup of whey, let all that vexes me be counted God's will.

Praying to you, O God, may my body's blood turn from anger.

I see on myself the shaggy cloak of age — no, I am wrong:

Grey is the hair that grows through my skin, like the lichen on an old tree.

The Old Woman (1910–11)
Paul Henry (1876–1958)

My right eye has been taken away, alienated for my forfeited estate,

And the left eye has been taken to complete its bankruptcy.

The flood wave, and the swift ebb;

What the flood brings to you the ebb carries out of your hand.

The flood wave, and the following ebb;

Both have come to me, so that I am well acquainted with them.

The flood wave has not reached my pantry; though my own visitors be many,

A hand has been laid on them all.

Well might the Son of Mary spend the night and be under the roof-tree of my pantry;

Though I am unable to offer any other hospitality,

I have never said 'No' to anybody.

God help anybody — man is the most miserable of creatures —

Whose ebb was not seen as his flood was seen.

Happy is the island of the great sea, for the flood comes to it after the ebb;

As for me, I expect no flood after ebb to come to me.

Translated by David Green and Frank O'Connor

THE FORT OF RATHANGAN

Anon

The fort over against the oak-wood,

Once it was Bruidge's, it was Cathal's,

It was Aed's, it was Ailill's,

It was Conaing's, it was Cuilíne's

And it was Maeldúin's;

The fort remains after each in his turn —

And the kings asleep in the ground.

Translated by Kuno Meyer

Two Girls Before a Ring Fort
George 'AE' Russell (1867–1935)

ONWARD, MY BARQUE
Bishop Patrick

Onward, my barque,
Through the long sea!
Christ on the water
Be thy steersman,
With sure oar
And a clear sky!

Hasten, my barque,
Through the hollow sea,
And cleave the pale
And horrid waves
Foam besprayed:
Sailor-like, steered by
A favouring breeze!

Onward, my book,
(Be an angel at thy side)
Through the wide sea:
To visit the dear home
Of Bishop Wulfstan!
Is he well
Who is worthy of honour,
Dear in love?

Drive sadness from him!
Sing forth joy
By day and night
With sweet voice,
Even to the sun,
To the topmost stars!

Hasten, my page,
By the holy strength
Of the high cross!
May thy sails swell
Through the clean waves!
Learn, my barque,
To run in safety
Through the fields of the sea!
Learn to be like unto
The dread monsters
Of the sea, by swimming
Through the bitter waters!

Onward, my book!
Though shalt go in joy
Through wind and wave.
The scale-clad throng

Shipping off Whitby (c.1830)
Frederick Calvert (1793–1852)

Shall keep thee company,
And the helmsman's cry
With sweet tone
Shall sound strongly
From the depths of the sea.

Hasten, my barque,
In joy through the waters!
May the tops of thy sail
Be swollen full
By the eastern breeze!
Without a cloud
May the breezes serve thee,
[Nor] may any error
O'erwhelm [thee]
Until thou art borne
On a straight course
To the fields of England!

Onward, my page!
In my thought following
I shall be thy companion.
I am drawn by love
To visit the dear
Fosterchildren of peace.
To all Christ's faithful
Of kind Bishop Wulfstan,
To them all equally
Bring, as is fitting,
Thrice ten greetings
In fair order!

Onward, my book,
With halting verse:
And from me, Patrick,
Loyal in memory,
Ask, as is fitting,
For my comrade Aldwin
A thousand crowns of blessed life!

Translated by R.S.

THE DAY OF WRATH
from the Latin of Saint Columba

Day of the king most righteous,
    The day is nigh at hand,
The day of wrath and vengeance,
    And darkness on the land.

Day of thick clouds and voices,
    Of mighty thundering,
A day of narrow anguish
    And bitter sorrowing.

The love of women's over,
    And ended is desire,
Men's strife with men is quiet
    And the world lusts no more.

Translated by Helen Waddell

Scene from the Apocalypse (1829)
Francis Danby (1793–1861)

AGAINST BLAME OF WOMAN

Gerald Fitzgerald, Earl of Desmond

Speak not ill of womankind,
 'Tis no wisdom if you do.
You that fault in women find,
 I would not be praised of you.

Sweetly speaking, witty, clear,
 Tribe most lovely to my mind,
Blame of such I hate to hear.
 Speak not ill of womankind.

Bloody treason, murderous act,
 Not by women were designed,
Bells o'erthrown nor churches sacked.
 Speak not ill of womankind.

Bishop, King upon his throne,
 Primate skilled to loose and bind,
Sprung of women every one!
 Speak not ill of womankind.

For a brave young fellow long
 Hearts of women oft have pined.
Who would dare their love to wrong?
 Speak not ill of womankind.

Paunchy greybeards never more
 Hope to please a woman's mind.
Poor young chieftains they adore!
 Speak not ill of womankind.

Version: Earl of Longford

The Falconer (1853)
Daniel Maclise (1806–1870)

THE KISS

Anon

Oh, keep your kisses, young provoking girl!
    I find no taste in any maiden's kiss.
Altho' your teeth be whiter than the pearl,
    I will not drink at fountains such as this.

I know a man whose wife did kiss my mouth
    With kiss more honeyed than the honeycomb.
And never another's kiss can slake my drought
    After that kiss, till judgment hour shall come.

Till I do gaze on her for whom I long,
    If ever God afford such grace to men,
I would not love a woman old or young,
    Till she do kiss me as she kissed me then.

Translated by the Earl of Longford

Affectionate Couple
Beatrice Glenavy (1881–1970)

MY HAND HAS A PAIN FROM WRITING

Anon

My hand has a pain from writing,
Not steady the sharp tool of my craft.
Its slender beak spews bright ink —
A beetle-dark shining draught.

Streams of wisdom of white God
from my fair-brown, fine hand sally,
On the page they splash their flood
In ink of the green-skinned holly.

My little dribbly pen stretches
Across the great white paper plain,
Insatiable for splendid riches —
That is why my hand has pain!

Translated by Flann O'Brien

Day Dreams
Francis Sylvester Walker (1848–1916)

CHRISTMAS DAY IS COME

Luke Wadding

Christmas Day is come; let's all prepare for mirth,
  Which fills the heav'ns and earth at this amazing birth.
Through both the joyous angels in strife and hurry fly,
  With glory and hosannas; 'All Holy' do they cry,
In heaven the Church triumphant adores with all her choirs,
  The militant on earth with humble faith admires.

But why should we rejoice? Should we not rather mourn
  To see the Hope of Nations thus in a stable born?
Where are His crown and sceptre, where is His throne sublime,
  Where is His train majestic that should the stars outshine?
Is there not sumptuous palace nor any inn at all
  To lodge His heav'nly mother but in a filthy stall?

Oh! Cease, ye blessed angels, such clamorous joys to make!
  Though midnight silence favours, the shepherds are awake;
And you, O glorious star! That with new splendour brings,
  From the remotest parts three learned eastern kings,
Turn somewhere else your luster, your rays elsewhere display,
  For Herod he may slay the babe, and Christ must straight away.

If we would then rejoice, let's cancel the old score,
  And purposing amendment, resolve to sin no more —
For mirth can ne'er content us, without a conscience clear;
  And thus we'll find true pleasure in all the usual cheer,
In dancing, sporting, revelling, with masquerade and drum,
  So let our Christmas merry be, as Christmas doth become.

The Dancing Master (c. *1848)*
Daniel MacDonald (1821–1853)

O it's Best be a Total Boor

Dáibhí Ó Bruadair

O it's best be a total boor
    (though it's bad be a boor at all)
if I'm to go out and about
    among these stupid people.

It's best to be, good people,
    a stutterer among you
since that is what you want,
    you blind ignorant crew.

If I found me a man to swap
    I'd give him my lovely skill.
He'd find it as good as a cloak
    around him against the gloom.

Since a man is respected more
    for his suit than for his talents
I regret what I've spent on my art,
    that I haven't it now in clothes.

Since happy in word and deed is each boorish clod
without music or metre or motherwit on his tongue,
I regret what I've wasted struggling with hard print
since the prime of life — that I might have spent as a boor.

Translated by Thomas Kinsella

St Patrick's Day (1867)
Charles Henry Cook (*c.*1830–*c.*1906)

KILCASH

Anon

What shall we do for timber?
  The last of the woods is down,
Kilcash and the house of its glory
  and the bell of the house are gone,
The spot where that lady waited
  that shamed all women for grace,
When earls came sailing to meet her
  and Mass was said in that place.

My grief and my affliction,
  your gates are taken away,
Your avenue needs attention,
  goats in the garden stray,
The courtyard's filled with water,
  and the great earls where are they?
The earls, the lady, the people
  beaten into the clay.

No sound of duck or geese there
  hawk's cry or eagle's call,
No humming of the bees there
  that brought honey and wax for all,
Nor even the gentle song of the birds there
  when the sun has gone down in the west,
Nor a cuckoo atop of the boughs there,
  singing the world to rest.

There's mist there tumbling from branches
  unstirred by night and by day,
And a darkness falling from heaven,
  and our fortunes have ebbed away;
There's no holly nor hazel nor ash there,
  the pasture is rock and stone,
The crown of the forest is withered
  and the last of its game is gone.

I beseech of Mary and Jesus
  that the great come home again,
With long dances danced in the garden,
  fiddle music and mirth among men,
That Kilcash, the home of our fathers,
  be lifted on high again,
And from that to the deluge of waters
  in bounty and peace remain.

Translated by Frank O'Connor

Dripsey Castle (c.1950)
Diarmuid O'Ceallachain (1915–1993)

WHILE SHEPHERDS WATCHED THEIR FLOCKS BY NIGHT

Nahum Tate

While shepherds watched their flocks by night,
 All seated on the ground,
The angel of the Lord came down,
 And glory shone around.

'Fear not,' said he, for mighty dread
 Had seized their troubled mind;
'Glad tidings of great joy I bring
 To you and all mankind.

'To you, in David's town, this day
 Is born of David's line,
The Saviour, who is Christ the Lord,
 And this shall be the sign:

'The heavenly babe you there shall find
 To human view displayed,
All meanly wrapped in swaddling bands,
 And in a manger laid.'

Thus spake the seraph; and forthwith
 Appeared a shining throng
Of angels, praising God, who thus
 Addressed their joyful song:

'All glory be to God on high,
 And to the earth be peace;
Good will henceforth from Heaven to men
 Begin and never cease.'

Mountain Sheep
Grace Henry (1863–1953)

from VERSES ON THE DEATH OF DR SWIFT

Jonathan Swift

The Time is not remote, when I
Must by the Course of Nature dye:
When I forsee my special Friends,
Will try to find their private Ends:
Tho' it is hardly understood,
Which way my Death can do them good;
Yet, thus methinks, I hear 'em speak;
See, how the Dean begins to break:
Poor Gentleman, he droops apace,
You plainly find it in his Face:
That old Vertigo in his Head,
Will never leave him, till he's dead:
Besides, his Memory decays,
He recollects not what he says;
He cannot call his Friends to Mind;
Forgets the Place where last he din'd:
Plyes you with Stories o'er and o'er,
He told them fifty Times before.
How does he fancy we can sit,
To hear his out-of-fashion'd Wit?
But he takes up with younger Fokes,
Who for his Wine will bear his Jokes:
Faith, he must make his Stories shorter,
Or change his Comrades once a Quarter:
In half the Time, he talks them round;
There must another Sett be found.

Jonathan Swift
Charles Jervas (*c.*1675–1739)

For Poetry, he's past his Prime,
He takes an Hour to find a Rhime:
His Fire is out, his Wit decay'd,
His Fancy sunk, his Muse a Jade.
I'd have him throw away his Pen;
But there's no talking to some Men.

And, then their Tenderness appears,
By adding largely to my Years:
'He's older than he would be reckon'd,
And well remembers Charles the Second.

'He hardly drinks a Pint of Wine;
And that, I doubt, is no good Sign.
His Stomach too begins to fail:
Last Year we thought him strong and hale;
But now, he's quite another Thing;
I wish he may hold out till Spring.'

Then hug themselves, and reason thus;
'It is not yet so bad with us.'

'Behold the fatal Day arrive!
How is the Dean? He's just alive.
Now the departing Prayer is read:
He hardly breathes. The Dean is dead.

Before the Passing-Bell begun,
The News thro' half the Town has run.
O, may we all for Death prepare!
What has he left? And who's his Heir?
I know no more than what the News is,
'Tis all bequeath'd to publick Uses.
To publick Use! A perfect Whim!
What had the Publick done for him!

'Mere Envy, Avarice, and Pride!
He gave it all: — But first he dy'd.
And had the Dean, in all the Nation,
No worthy Friend, no poor Relation?
So ready to do Strangers good,
Forgetting his own Flesh and Blood?'

From Dublin soon to London spread,
'Tis told at Court, the Dean is dead.

Kind Lady Suffolk in the Spleen,
Runs laughing up to tell the Queen.
The Queen, so Gracious, Mild, and Good,
Cries, 'Is he gone? 'Tis time he shou'd.
He's dead you say; why let him rot;
I'm glad the Medals were forgot.

I promis'd them, I own; but when?
I only was the Princess then;
But now as Consort of the King,
You know 'tis quite a different Thing.'

The rest will give a Shrug and cry
I'm sorry; but we all must dye.
Indifference clad in Wisdom's Guise,
All Fortitude of Mind supplies:
For how can stony Bowels melt,
In those who never Pity felt;
When *We* are lash'd, *They* kiss the Rod;
Resigning to the Will of God.

My female Friends, whose tender Hearts
Have better learn'd to act their Parts.
Receive the News in doleful Dumps,
'The Dean is dead, (and what is Trumps?)
Then Lord have Mercy on his Soul.
(Ladies I'll venture for the Vole.)
Six Deans they say must bear the Pall.
(I wish I knew what King to call.)
Madam, your Husband will attend
The Funeral of so good a Friend.
No, Madam, 'tis a shocking Sight,
And he's engag'd To-morrow Night!

My Lady Club wou'd take it ill,
If he shou'd fail her at Quadrille.
He lov'd the Dean. (I lead a Heart.)
But dearest Friends, they say, must part.
His Time was come; he ran his Race;
We hope he's in a better Place.'

'Perhaps I may allow, the Dean
Had too much Satyr in his Vein;
And seem'd determin'd not to starve it,
Because no Age could more deserve it.
Yet, Malice never was his Aim;
He lash'd the Vice but spar'd the Name.
No Individual could resent,
Where Thousands equally were meant.
'He gave the little Wealth he had,
To build a House for Fools and Mad:
And shew'd by one satyric Touch,
No Nation wanted it so much:
That Kingdom he hath left his Debtor,
I wish it soon may have a Better.'

LAST LINES

Egan O'Rahilly

I shall not call for help until they coffin me —
What good for me to call when hope of help is gone?
Princes of Munster who would have heard my cry
Will not rise from the dead because I am alone.

Mind shudders like a wave in this tempestuous mood,
My bowels and my heart are pierced and filled with pain
To see our lands, our hills, our gentle neighbourhood,
A plot where any English upstart stakes his claim.

The Shannon and the Liffey and the tuneful Lee,
The Boyne and the Black Water a sad music sing,
The waters of the west run red into the sea —
No matter what be trumps, their knave will beat our King.

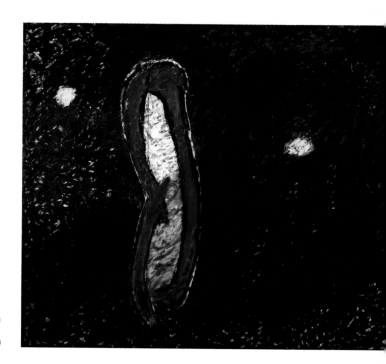

Image from a Remote Silence (c. 1990)
Mick Mulcahy (1952–)

And I can never cease weeping these useless tears;

I am a man oppressed, afflicted and undone.

Who where he wanders mourning no companion hears

Only some waterfall that has no cause to mourn.

Now I shall cease; death comes, and I must not delay.

By Laune and Laine and Lee, diminished of their pride,

I shall go after the heroes, aye, into the clay —

My fathers followed theirs before Christ was crucified.

Translated by Frank O'Connor

Banks of the River Shannon
Geraldine M. O'Brien (1922–)

Grief
Jack Butler Yeats (1871–1957)

THE BEAU WALK IN STEPHEN'S GREEN

Thomas Newburgh

'Mid Trees of stunted Growth, unequal Roes,

On the coarse Gravel, trip the Belles and Beaus.

Here, on one Side, extends a length of Street,

Where Dirt-bespattering Cars and Coaches meet.

On t'other, in the Ditches lazy Flood,

Dead Cats and Dogs lie bloated; drench'd in Mud.

But lo! a Statue from afar salutes your Eyes,

To which th'Inclosure all Access denies.

So distant, whose, or whom, no Eye can ken,

Plac'd in the Centre of a marshy Fen.

But know, 'tis Royal George on whom you stare,

Tho' oft mistaken for some good Lord Mayor:

And tho' his Charger foams in ductile Brass,

The Charger for an ambling Pad may pass;

The whole equestrian Statue for a Toy,

A Horse of Hobby, mounted by a Boy.

For shame ye Cits, where meet th'assembl'd Fair,

Fill up your Dikes and purge th'unwholsome Air.

Let George's royal Form be fairly shewn,

And like his Virtues, be reveal'd and known.

St Stephen's Green
Harry Kernoff (1900–1974)

ELEGY ON THE DEATH OF A MAD DOG

Oliver Goldsmith

Good people all, of every sort,
    Give ear unto my song;
And if you find it wond'rous short,
    It cannot hold you long.

In Islington there was a man,
    Of whom the world might say,
That still a godly race he ran,
    Whene'er he went to pray.

A kind and gentle heart he had,
    To comfort friends and foes;
The naked every day he clad,
    When he put on his clothes.

And in that town a dog was found,
    As many dogs there be,
Both mongrel, puppy, whelp, and hound,
    And curs of low degree.

This dog and man at first were friends;
    But when a pique began,
The dog, to gain some private ends,
    Went mad and bit the man.

Around from all the neighbouring streets
    The wond'ring neighbours ran,
And swore the dog had lost his wits,
    To bite so good a man.

The wound it seem'd both sore and sad
    To every Christian eye;
And while they swore the dog was mad,
    They swore the man would die.

But soon a wonder came to light,
    That show'd the rogues they lied:
The man recover'd of the bite,
    The dog it was that died.

Painting of a Dog (1952)
Francis Bacon (1909–1992)

Ill Fares the Land *from* The Deserted Village

Oliver Goldsmith

Ill fares the land, to hast'ning ills a prey,
Where wealth accumulates, and men decay:
Princes and lords may flourish, or may fade;
A breath can make them, as a breath has made;
But a bold peasantry, their country's pride,
When once destroy'd, can never be supplied.

A time there was, ere England's griefs began,
When every rood of ground maintain'd its man;
For him light labour spread her wholesome store,
Just gave what life requir'd, but gave no more:
His best companions, innocence and health;
And his best riches, ignorance of wealth.

But times are alter'd; trade's unfeeling train
Usurp the land and dispossess the swain;
Along the lawn, where scatter'd hamlets rose,
Unwieldy wealth, and cumbrous pomp repose;
And every want to opulence allied,
And every pang that folly pays to pride.
Those gentle hours that plenty bade to bloom,
Those calm desires that ask'd but little room,
Those healthful sports that grac'd the peaceful scene,
Liv'd in each look, and brighten'd all the green, —
These, far departing, seek a kinder shore,
And rural mirth and manners are no more.

Deserted Village
Robert Ryan (1964–)

THE RAKES OF MALLOW

Anon

Beauing, belling, dancing, drinking,
Breaking windows, cursing, sinking,
Ever raking, never thinking,
   Live the Rakes of Mallow,

Spending faster than it comes,
Beating waiter's bailiffs, duns,
Bacchus' true begotten sons,
   Live the Rakes of Mallow.

One time naught but claret drinking,
Then like politicians, thinking
To raise the sinking funds when sinking.
   Live the Rakes of Mallow.

When at home with dadda dying,
Still for Mallow-water crying,
But where there's good claret plying
   Live the rakes of Mallow.

Living short but merry lives,
Going where the devil drives,
Having sweethearts, but no wives,
   Live the rakes of Mallow.

Racking tenants, stewards teasing,
Swiftly spending, slowly raising,
Wishing to spend all their lives in
   Raking as at Mallow.

Then to end this raking life,
They get sober, take a wife,
Ever after live in strife,
   And wish again for Mallow.

A Bird Never Flew on One Wing
Harry Kernoff (1900–1974)

from THE LAMENT FOR ART O'LEARY

Eibhlín Dhubh Ní Chonaill

My love forever!
The day I first saw you
At the end of the market-house,
My eye observed you,
My heart approved you,
I fled from my father with you,
Far from my home with you.

I never repented it:
You whitened a parlour for me,
Painted rooms for me,
Reddened ovens for me,
Baked fine bread for me,
Basted meat for me,
Slaughtered beasts for me;
I slept in ducks' feathers
Till midday milking-time
Or more if it pleased me.

My friend forever!
My mind remembers
That fine spring day
How well your hat suited you,
Bright gold-banded,
Sword silver-hilted —
Right hand steady —
Threatening aspect —
Trembling terror
On treacherous enemy —
You poised for a canter
On your slender bay horse.
The Saxons bowed to you,
Down to the ground to you,
Not for love of you
But for deadly fear of you,
Though you lost your life to them,
Oh my soul's darling.

Oh white-handed rider!
How fine your brooch was
Fastened in cambric,
And your hat with laces
When you crossed the sea to us,
They would clear the street for you,
And not for love of you
But for deadly hatred.

My friend you were forever!
When they will come home to me,
Gentle little Conor
And Farr O'Leary, the baby,
They will question me so quickly,
Where did I leave their father.
I'll answer in my anguish
That I left him in Killnamartyr.
They will call out to their father:
And he won't be there to answer.

A Lament for Art O'Leary (1940)
Jack Butler Yeats (1871–1957)

My friend and my love!
Of the blood of Lord Antrim,
And of Barry of Allchoill,
How well your sword suited you,
Hat gold-banded,
Boots of fine leather,
Coat of broadcloth,
Spun overseas for you.

My friend you were forever!
I knew nothing of your murder
Till your horse came to the stable
With the reins beneath her trailing,
And your heart's blood on her shoulders
Staining the tooled saddle
Where you used to sit and stand.
My first leap reached the threshold,
My second reached the gateway,
My third leap reached the saddle.

I struck my hands together
And I made the bay horse gallop
As fast as I was able,
Till I found you dead before me
Beside a little furze-bush.
Without Pope or bishop,
Without priest or cleric
To read the death-psalms for you,
But a spent old woman only
Who spread her cloak to shroud you —
Your heart's blood was still flowing;
I did not stay to wipe it
But filled my hands and drank it.

Translated by Eilís Dillon

The Sad Girl (1923)
Sarah Purser (1848–1943)

JINGLE

John O'Keeffe

Amo, amas,
I love a lass
As cedar tall and slender;
Sweet cowslip's face
Is her nominative case,
And she's of the feminine gender.
Rorum, corum, sunt divorum!
Harum, scarum Divo!
Tag rag, merry derry, periwig and bobtail,
Hic hac, horum genetivo!

Can I decline
A nymph divine?
Her voice as a flute is *dulcis*!
Her *oculi* bright!
Her *manus* white!
And soft, when I *tacto*, her pulse is!
Rorum, corum, sunt divorum!
Harum, scarum Divo!
Tag rag, merry derry, periwig and bobtail,
Hic hac, horum genetivo!

O, how *bella*
Is my *puella*!
I'll kiss *sæculorum*
If I've luck, sir.
She's my *uxor*.
O, dies benedictorum!
Rorum, corum, sunt divorum!
Harum, scarum Divo!
Tag rag, merry derry, periwig and bobtail,
Hic hac, horum genetivo!

Dreams (1863)
Frederick William Burton (1816–1900)

from THE MIDNIGHT COURT
Brian Merriman

But you see the troubles a man takes on;
From the minute he marries his peace is gone,
Forever in fear of a neighbour's sneer,
And my own experience cost me dear.
I lived alone as happy as Larry,
Till I took it into my head to marry;
Tilling my fields with an easy mind
And going wherever I felt inclined,
Welcomed by all as a man of price,
Always ready with good advice;
The neighbours listened, they couldn't refuse
For I'd money and stock to uphold my views;
Everything came at my beck and call
Till a woman appeared and destroyed it all.
A beautiful girl with a ripening bosom,
Cheeks as bright as apple-blossom,
Hair that glimmered and foamed in the wind
And a face that blazed with the light behind,
A tinkling laugh and a modest carriage
And a twinkling eye that was ripe for marriage.
I goggled and gaped like one born mindless
Till I took her face for a form of kindness,
Though that wasn't quite what the Lord intended
For He marked me down like a man offended

For a vengence that wouldn't be easy mended
With my folly exposed and my comfort ended.

This girl was poor, she hadn't a home,
Hadn't a thing to call her own;
Drifting about, ignored, despised,
Doing odd jobs for other men's wives;
As if for drudgery created
Begging a crust from women she hated.
He pretended her troubles were over,
Married to him she'd live in clover;
The cows she milked would be her own,
The feather bed and the decent home;
The sack of turf, the lamp to light,
The sodded wall of a winter's night;
Flax and wool to weave and wind,
The womanly things for which she pined.
Even his friends could not have said
That his looks were such that she lost her head.
How else would he come by such a wife
But that ease was the alms she asked of life?
What possible use could she have at night
For dourness, dropsy, bother and blight,
A basket of bones with thighs of lead,

The Beggar Girl
William Orpen (1878–1931)

Knees absconded from the dead,
Reddening shanks and temples whitening,
Looking like one that was struck by lightning?
Is there living a girl that could grow fat
Tied to a travelling corpse like that;
Who twice a year wouldn't find a wish
To see what was she, flesh or fish,
But dragged the clothes about his head
Like a wintry wind to a woman in bed?

Was it too much to expect as right
A little attention once a night?
From all I know she was never accounted
A woman too modest to be mounted;
Gentle, good-humoured and God-fearing,
We need never suppose she denied her rearing.
Whatever the lengths his fancy ran
She wouldn't take fright from a mettlesome man,
And would sooner a boy would be aged a score
Than himself on the job for a week or more;
And dancing at night or Mass at morning,
Fiddle or flute or choir or organ,
She'd sooner the tune that boy would play
As midnight struck or at break of day.

Damn it, you know we're all the same,
A woman nine months in terror and pain,
The minute that Death has lost the game —
Good morrow, my love, and she's off again!
And then imagine what 'twas like
With a creature like that in the bed at night
That never came close in a friendly way
From All Souls' Night to St Brigid's Day!
You'd all agree 'twas a horrible fate —
Sixty winters on his pate;
An old dead tree with its timbers drained
And a twenty year old with her heart untamed.
It wasn't her fault if things went wrong;
She closed her eyes and held her tongue;
She was no querulous, restless, bawling,
Rearing, leaping, pinching, scrawling,
Hussy from school that smooth and warm
Cushioned him like a sheaf of corn.
Line by line she bade him linger
With gummy lips and groping finger;
Gripping his thighs in a wild embrace,
Rubbing her brush from knee to waist,
Stripping him bare to the cold night air,

Everything that a woman would dare;

But she'd nothing to show for all her pain,

His bleary old eyes looked just the same;

And nothing I said could ever explain

Her sum of misery and shame

Her knees in the air and the clothes beneath her,

Chattering teeth and limbs in fever,

As she sobbed and tossed through a joyless night

And gave it up with the morning light.

Translated by Frank O'Connor

The Charity of the Poor
Francis Sylvester Walker (1848–1916)

LET THE TOAST PASS

Richard Brinsley Sheridan

Here's to the maiden of bashful fifteen,
    Here's to the widow of fifty;
Here's to the flaunting, extravagant queen,
    And here's to the housewife that's thrifty.
        Let the toast pass,
        Drink to the lass,
I'll warrant she'll prove an excuse for the glass.

Here's to the charmer whose dimples we prize,
    Now to the maid who has none, sir,
Here's to the girl with a pair of blue eyes,
    And here's to the nymph with but one, sir!
        Let the toast pass,
        Drink to the lass,
I'll warrant she'll prove an excuse for the glass.

Here's to the maid with a bosom of snow,
    And to her that's as brown as a berry;
Here's to the wife, with a face full of woe,
    And now to the damsel that's merry:
        Let the toast pass,
        Drink to the lass,
I'll warrant she'll prove an excuse for the glass.

For let 'em be clumsy, or let 'em be slim,
    Young or ancient, I care not a feather;
So fill the pint bumper quite up to the brim,
And let us e'en toast them together:
        Let the toast pass,
        Drink to the lass,
I'll warrant she'll prove an excuse for the glass.

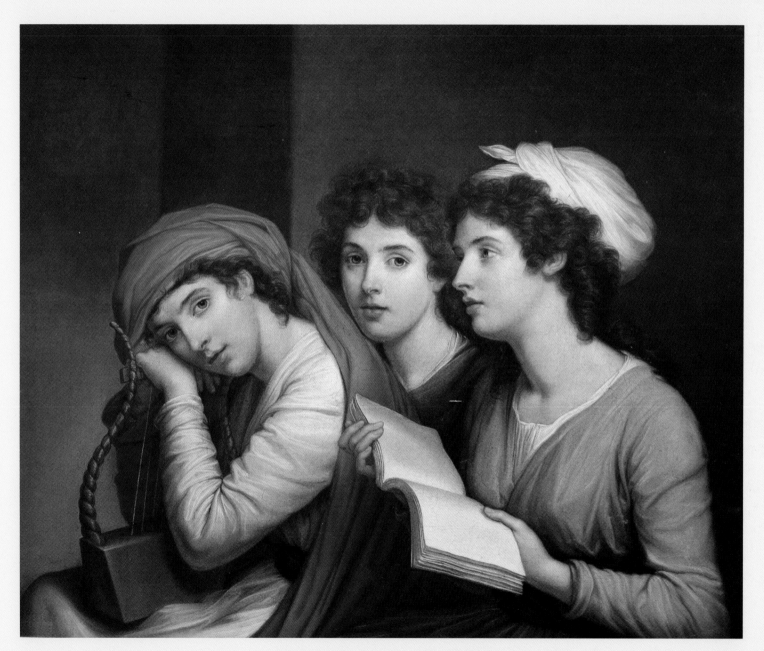

Lady Hamilton as the Three Muses
Hugh Douglas Hamilton (*c.*1734–1808)

THE WAKE OF WILLIAM ORR

William Drennan

Here our murdered brother lies:
Wake him not with women's cries;
Mourn the way that manhood ought;
Sit in silent trance of thought.

Write his merits on your mind:
Morals pure and manners kind;
In his head, as on a hill,
Virtue placed her citadel.

Why cut off in palmy youth?
Truth he spoke, and acted truth:
'Countrymen, unite!' he cried,
And died – for what his Saviour died.

God of Peace, and God of Love,
Let it not thy vengeance move,
Let it not thy lightnings draw, –
A nation guillotined by law!

Hapless nation! rent and torn,
Thou wert early taught to mourn,
Warfare of six hundred years –
Epochs marked with blood and tears!

Hunted through thy native grounds,
Or flung reward to human hounds;
Each one pulled and tore his share,
Heedless of thy deep despair.

Hapless nation – hapless land,
Heap of uncementing sand
Crumbled by a foreign weight;
And by worse – domestic hate.

God of mercy! God of peace!
Make the mad confusion cease;
O'er the mental chaos move,
Through it speak the light of love.

Monstrous and unhappy sight!
Brothers' blood will not unite;
Holy oil and holy water
Mix, and fill the world with slaughter.

Who is she with aspect wild?
The widowed mother with her child,
Child new stirring in the womb,
Husband waiting for the tomb!

Angel of this sacred place,
Calm her soul and whisper peace;
Cord, or axe, or guillotine
Make the sentence – not the sin.

Here we watch our brother's sleep:
Watch with us, but do not weep;
Watch with us through dead of night,
But expect the morning light.

Conquer fortune – persevere! –
Lo! it breaks, the morning clear!
The cheerful cock awakes the skies,
The day is come – arise! – arise!

The End, or Not Your Turn Yet (1950s)
Gerard Dillon (1916–1971)

SHE IS FAR FROM THE LAND

Thomas Moore

She is far from the land where her young hero sleeps,
    And lovers are round her, sighing:
But coldly she turns from their gaze, and weeps,
    For her heart in his grave is lying.

She sings the wild song of her dear native plains,
    Every note which he lov'd awaking; —
Ah! little they think who delight in her strains,
    How the heart of the Minstrel is breaking.

He had liv'd for his love, for his country he died,
    They were all that to life had entwin'd him;
Nor soon shall the tears of his country be dried,
    Nor long will his love stay behind him.

Oh! make her a grave where the sunbeams rest,
    When they promise a glorious morrow;
They'll shine o'er her sleep, like a smile from the West,
    From her own lov'd island of sorrow.

Connemara Lovers
Gerard Dillon (1916–1971)

THE CROPPY BOY

Anon

'Twas early, early in the spring,
The birds did whistle and sweetly sing,
Changing their notes from tree to tree,
And the song they sang was Old Ireland free.

'Twas early, early in the night,
The yeoman cavalry gave me a fright;
The yeoman cavalry was my downfall
And taken was I by Lord Cornwall.

'Twas in the guard-house that I was laid
And in a parlour that I was tried;
My sentence passed and my courage low
To new Geneva I was forced to go.

As I was passing by my father's door,
My brother William stood on the floor;
My aged father stood at the door,
And my tender mother her hair she tore.

As I was walking up Wexford Street
My own first cousin I chanced to meet;
My own first cousin did me betray,
And for one bare guinea swore my life away.

As I was walking up Wexford Hill,
Who could blame me if I cried my fill?
I looked behind and I looked before,
But my tender mother I could see no more.

As I was mounted on the platform high,
My aged father was standing by;
My aged father did me deny,
And the name he gave me was the Croppy Boy.

It was in Geneva this young man died,
And in Geneva his body lies;
And you good Christians that do pass by
Shed just one tear for the Croppy Boy.

Portrait of a Youth
William Orpen (1878–1931)

I am Raftery

Antoine Ó Raifteiri

I am Raftery the poet,
    Full of hope and love,
With eyes that have no light,
    With gentleness that has no misery.

Going west upon my pilgrimage
    Guided by the light of my heart,
Feeble and tired,
    To the end of my road.

Behold me now,
    And my face to a wall,
A-playing music
    Unto empty pockets.

Translated by Douglas Hyde

Fiddle Player
J.B. Vallely (1941–)

THE FINDING OF MOSES

Zozimus (Michael Moran)

On Egypt's banks, contagious to the Nile
The auld Pharaoh's daughter, she went to bathe in style.
She took her dip and she came unto the land,
And to dry her royal pelt she ran along the strand.
A bulrush tripped her, whereupon she saw
A smiling babby in a wad of straw.
She took him up and says she in accents mild,
'Oh tar-an-a-gers, now me girls, which one of yis
    owns the child?'

She took him up and she gave a little grin
For she and Moses were standing in their skin;
'Bedad now,' says she, 'it was someone very rude
Left a little baby by the river in his nude.'
She took him to her auld lad sitting on the throne;
'Da,' says she, 'will you give the boy a home?'
'Bedad now,' says he, 'sure I've often brought in worse.
Go my darling daughter and get the child a nurse.'

An auld blackamore woman among the crew
Cried out, 'You royal savage, what's that to do with you?
Your royal ladies is too meek and mild
To beget dishonestly this darling little child.'
'Ah then,' says the Pharaoh, 'I'll search every nook
From the Phoenix Park down to Donnybrook,
And when I catch a hoult of the bastard's father
I will kick him from the Nile down to the Dodder.'

Well they sent a bellman to the market square
To see if he could find a slavey there,
But the only one now that he could find
Was the little young one that left the child behind.
She came up to the Pharaoh, a stranger, mareyah,
Never lettin' on that she was the baby's ma.
And so little Moses got his mammy back,
Which shows that coincidence is a nut to crack.

Boat in Reeds (1999)
Anna Marie Dowdican (1969–)

THE OLD ORANGE FLUTE

Anon

In the County Tyrone, near the town of Dungannon,
Where many the ructions meself had a hand in,
Bob Williamson lived, a weaver by trade,
And all of us thought him a stout Orange blade.
On the Twelfth of July as it yearly did come,
Bob played with his flute to the sound of a drum.
You may talk of your harp, your piano or lute,
But none can compare with the Old Orange Flute.

Bob, the deceiver, he took us all in;
He married a Papist named Bridget McGinn.
Turned Papist himself and forsook the old cause
That gave us our freedom, religion and laws.
Now, boys of the townland made some noise upon it,
And Bob had to fly to the province of Connaught.
He fled with his wife and his fixings to boot,
And along with the latter his Old Orange Flute.

At the chapel on Sunday to atone for past deeds,
He'd say *Pater* and *Aves* and counted his brown beads.
'Til after some time, at the priest's own desire
He went with that old flute to play in the choir.
He went with that old flute for to play for the Mass,
But the instrument shivered and sighed, 'Oh, alas',
And try though he would, though it made a great noise,
The flute would play only 'The Protestant Boys'.

Bob jumped and he stared and got in a flutter

And threw the old flute in the blessed holy water.

He thought that this charm would bring some other sound;

When he tried it again, it played 'Croppies Lie Down'.

Now, for all he could whistle and finger and blow,

To play Papish music he found it no go.

'Kick the Pope' and 'The Boyne Water' it freely would sound,

But one Papish squeak in it couldn't be found.

At a council of priests that was held the next day

They decided to banish the old flute away;

They couldn't knock heresy out of its head,

So they bought Bob another to play in its stead.

And the old flute was doomed, and its fate was pathetic,

'Twas fastened and burnt at the stake as heretic.

As the flames rose around it, you could hear a strange noise

'Twas the old flute still a-whistlin' 'The Protestant Boys'.

The Flute Player
Leo Whelan (1892–1956)

A Vision of Connaught in the Thirteenth Century

James Clarence Mangan

I walked entranced
    Through a land of Morn;
The sun, with wondrous excess of light,
    Shone down and glanced
    Over seas of corn
And lustrous gardens aleft and right.
    Even in the clime
    Of resplendent Spain,
Beams no such sun upon such a land;
    But it was the time,
    'Twas in the reign,
Of Cáhal Mór of the Wine-red Hand.

Anon stood nigh
    By my side a man
Of princely aspect and port sublime.
    Him queried I —
    'O, my Lord and Khan,
What clime is this, and what golden time?'
    When he — 'The clime
    Is a clime to praise,
The clime is Erin's, the green and bland;
    And it is the time,
    These be the days,
Of Cáhal Mór of the Wine-red Hand!'

Then saw I thrones,
    And circling fires,
And a Dome rose near me, as by a spell,
    Whence flowed the tones
    Of silver lyres,
And many voices in wreathèd swell;
    And their thrilling chime
    Fell on mine ears
As the heavenly hymn of an angel-band —
    'It is now the time,
    These be the years,
Of Cáhal Mór of the Wine-red Hand!'

I sought the hall,
    And, behold! — a change
From light to darkness, from joy to woe!
    King, nobles, all,
    Looked aghast and strange;
The minstrel-group sate in dumbest show!
    Had some great crime
    Wrought this dread amaze,
This terror? None seemed to understand
    'Twas then the time,
    We were in the days,
Of Cáhal Mór of the Wine-red Hand.

I again walked forth;
But lo! the sky
Showed fleckt with blood, and an alien sun
Glared from the north,
And there stood on high,
Amid his shorn beams, a skeleton!
It was by the stream
Of the castled Maine,
One Autumn eve, in the Teuton's land,
That I dreamed this dream
Of the time and reign
Of Cáhal Mór of the Wine-red Hand!

Loisceadh Fiaileach, Ruis Eo (c.1950)
Patrick Leonard (1918–2005)

A Song from the Coptic

James Clarence Mangan

Quarrels have long been in vogue among sages;
    Still, though in many things wranglers and rancourous,
All the philosopher-scribes of all ages
    Join, *una voce*, on one point to anchor us.
Here is the gist of their mystified pages,
Here is the wisdom we purchase with gold —
Children of Light, leave the world to its mulishness,
Things to their natures, and fools to their foolishness;
Berries were bitter in forests of old.

Hoary old Merlin, that great necromancer,
Made me, a student, a similar answer,
When I besought him for light and for lore:
Toiler in vain! leave the world to its mulishness,
Things to their natures, and fools to their foolishness;
Granite was hard in the quarries of yore.

And on the ice-crested heights of Armenia,
And in the valleys of broad Abyssinia,
Still spake the Oracle just as before:
Wouldst thou have peace, leave the world to its mulishness,
Things to their natures and fools to their foolishness;
Beetles were blind in the ages of yore.

The Kingdom of Kerry (c.1925)
John Lavery (1856–1941)

THE BELLS OF SHANDON

Francis Sylvester Mahony ('Father Prout')

With deep affection and recollection
   I often think of the Shandon bells,
Whose sounds so wild would, in days of childhood,
   Fling round my cradle their magic spells.
On this I ponder, where'er I wander,
   And thus grow fonder, sweet Cork, of thee,
      With thy bells of Shandon,
      That sound so grand on
The pleasant waters of the river Lee.

I have heard bells chiming full many a clime in,
   Tolling sublime in cathedral shrine;
While at a glib rate brass tongues would vibrate,
   But all their music spoke nought to thine;
For memory, dwelling on each proud swelling
   Of the belfry knelling its bold notes free,
      Made the bells of Shandon
      Sound far more grand on
The pleasant waters of the River Lee.

I have heard bells tolling 'old Adrian's mole' in,
   Their thunder rolling from the Vatican,
With cymbals glorious, swinging uproarious
   In the gorgeous turrets of Notre Dame;
But thy sounds were sweeter than the dome of Peter
   Flings o'er the Tiber, pealing solemnly.
      Oh! the bells of Shandon
      Sound far more grand on
The pleasant waters of River Lee.

There's a bell in Moscow, while on tower and Kiosk, O!
   In St Sophia the Turkman gets,
And loud in the air calls men to prayer
   From the tapering summit of tall minarets.
Such empty phantom I freely grant 'em,
   But there's an anthem more dear to me:
      'Tis the bells of Shandon,
      That sound so grand on
The pleasant waters of the River Lee.

Shandon (c. *1900)*
Lady Kate Dobbin (1868–1955)

A Nation Once Again

Thomas Davis

When boyhood's fire was in my blood,
  I read of ancient freemen,
For Greece and Rome who bravely stood,
  Three Hundred men and Three men.
And then I prayed I yet might see
  Our fetters rent in twain,
And Ireland, long a province, be
  A Nation once again.

And, from that time, through wildest woe,
  That hope has shone, a far light;
Nor could love's brightest summer glow
  Outshine that solemn starlight:
It seemed to watch above my head
  In forum, field, and fane;
Its angel voice sang round my bed,
  'A Nation once again'.

It whispered, too, that 'freedom's ark
  And service high and holy,
Would be profaned by feelings dark,
  And passions vain or lowly;
For freedom comes from God's right hand,
  And needs a godly train;
And righteous men must make our land
  A Nation once again.'

So, as I grew from boy to man,
  I bent me to that bidding—
My spirit of each selfish plan
  And cruel passion ridding;
For, thus I hoped some day to aid—
  Oh! can such hope be vain?
When my dear country shall be made
  A Nation once again.

Military Manoeuvres (1891)
Richard Thomas Moynan (1856–1906)

THE NIGHT BEFORE LARRY WAS STRETCHED

Anon

The night before Larry was stretched,
The boys they all paid him a visit;
A bait in their sacks, too, they fetched;
They sweated their duds till they riz it:
For Larry was ever the lad,
When a boy was condemned to the squeezer,
Would fence all the duds that he had
To help a poor friend to a sneezer,
And warm his gob 'fore he died.

The boys they came crowding in fast,
They drew all their stools round about him,
Six glims round his trap-case were placed,
He couldn't be well waked without 'em.
When one of us asked could he die
Without having truly repented,
Says Larry, 'That's all in my eye;
And first by the clargy invented,
To get a fat bit for themselves.'

'I'm sorry, dear Larry,' says I,
'To see you in this situation;
And, blister my limbs if I lie,
I'd as lieve it had been my own station.'
'Ochone! it's all over,' says he,
'For the neckcloth I'll be forced to put on,
And by this time tomorrow you'll see
Your poor Larry as dead as a mutton,
Because, why, his courage was good.

'And I'll be cut up like a pie,
And my nob from my body be parted.'
'You're in the wrong box, then,' says I,
'For blast me if they're so hard-hearted:
A chalk on the back of your neck
Is all that Jack Ketch dares to give you;
Then mind not such trifles a feck,
For why should the likes of them grieve you?
And now, boys, come tip us the deck.'

The cards being called for, they played,
Till Larry found one of them cheated;
A dart at his napper he made
(The boy being easily heated):
'Oh, by the hokey, you thief,
I'll scuttle your nob with my daddle!
You cheat me because I'm in grief,
But soon I'll demolish your noddle,
And leave you your claret to drink.'

Then the clergy came in with his book,
He spoke him so smooth and so civil;
Larry tipped him a Kilmainham look,
And pitched his big wig to the devil;
Then sighing, he threw back his head
To get a sweet drop of the bottle,
And pitiful sighing, he said:
'Oh, the hemp will be soon round my throttle
And choke my poor windpipe to death.

'Though sure it's the best way to die,
Oh, the devil a better a-livin'!
For, sure, when the gallows is high
Your journey is shorter to Heaven:
But what harasses Larry the most,
And makes his poor soul melancholy,
Is to think of the time when his ghost
Will come in a sheet to sweet Molly –
Oh, sure it will kill her alive!'

So moving these last words he spoke,
We all vented our tears in a shower;
For my part, I thought my heart broke,
To see him cut down like a flower.
On his travels we watched him next day;
Oh, the throttler! l thought I could kill him;
But Larry not one word did say,
Nor changed till he come to 'King William' –
Then, *musha!* his colour grew white.

When he came to the nubbling chit,
He was tucked up so neat and so pretty,
The rumbler jogged off from his feet,
And he died with his face to the city;
He kicked, too – but that was all pride,
For soon you might see 'twas all over;
Soon after the noose was untied,
And at darky we waked him in clover,
And sent him to take a ground sweat.

A Dispute Over Cards
Robert Lucius West (1774–1850)

THE MEMORY OF THE DEAD

John Kells Ingram

Who fears to speak of Ninety-eight?
Who blushes at the name?
When cowards mock the patriot's fate,
Who hangs his head for shame?
He's all a knave, or half a slave,
Who slights his country thus;
But a true man, like you, man,
Will fill your glass with us.

We drink the memory of the brave,
The faithful and the few;
Some lie far off beyond the wave,
Some sleep in Ireland, too;
All, all are gone; but still lives on
The fame of those who died;
All true men, like you, men,
Remember them with pride.

Some on the shores of distant lands
Their weary hearts have laid,
And by the stranger's heedless hands
Their lonely graves were made;
But though their clay be far away
Beyond the Atlantic foam,
In true men, like you, men,
Their spirit's still at home.

The dust of some is Irish earth,
Among their own they rest,
And the same land that gave them birth
Has caught them to her breast;
And we will pray that from their clay
Full many a race may start
Of true men, like you, men,
To act as brave a part.

They rose in dark and evil days
To right their native land;
They kindled here a living blaze
That nothing shall withstand.
Alas! that might can vanquish right—
They fell and passed away;
But true men, like you, men,
Are plenty here to-day.

Then here's their memory — may it be
For us a guiding light,
To cheer our strife for liberty,
And teach us to unite—
Through good and ill, be Ireland's still,
Though sad as theirs your fate,
And true men be you, men,
Like those of Ninety-eight.

'Irish Rebellion' Panel (c.1934)
Richard King (1907–1974), Harry Clarke Studios

THE EVICTION *from* LAURENCE BLOOMFIELD IN IRELAND

William Allingham

In early morning twilight, raw and chill,
Damp vapours brooding on the barren hill,
Through miles of mire in steady grave array
Threescore well-arm'd police pursue their way;
Each tall and bearded man a rifle swings,
And under each greatcoat a bayonet clings;
The Sheriff on his sturdy cob astride
Talks with the chief, who marches by their side,
And, creeping on behind them, Paudeen Dhu
Pretends his needful duty much to rue.
Six big-boned labourers, clad in common frieze,
Walk in the midst, the Sheriff's staunch allies;
Six crowbar men, from distant county brought, —
Orange, and glorying in their work, 'tis thought,
But wrongly, — churls of Catholics are they,
And merely hired at half a crown a day.

The hamlet clustering on its hill is seen,
A score of petty homesteads, dark and mean;
Poor always, not despairing until now;
Long used, as well as poverty knows how,
With life's oppressive trifles to contend.
This day will bring its history to an end.
Moveless and grim against the cottage walls
Lean a few silent men: but someone calls

Far off; and then a child 'without a stitch'
Runs out of doors, flies back with piercing screech,
And soon from house to house is heard the cry
Of female sorrow, swelling loud and high,
Which makes the men blaspheme between their teeth.
Meanwhile, o'er fence and watery field beneath,
The little army moves through drizzling rain;
A 'Crowbar' leads the Sheriff's nag; the lane
Is enter'd, and their plashing tramp draws near;
One instant, outcry holds its breath to hear;
'Halt!' — at the doors they form in double line,
And ranks of polish'd rifles wetly shine.

The Sheriff's painful duty must be done;
He begs for quiet — and the work's begun.
The strong stand ready; now appear the rest,
Girl, matron, grandsire, baby on the breast,
And Rosy's thin face on a pallet borne;
A motley concourse, feeble and forlorn.
One old man, tears upon his wrinkled cheek,
Stands trembling on a threshold, tries to speak,
But, in defect of any word for this,
Mutely upon the doorpost prints a kiss,
Then passes out for ever. Through the crowd
The children run bewilder'd, wailing loud;

Eviction Scene (c. 1850)
Daniel MacDonald (1821–1853)

Where needed most, the men combine their aid;
And, last of all, is Oona forth convey'd,
Reclined in her accustom'd strawen chair,
Her aged eyelids closed, her thick white hair
Escaping from her cap; she feels the chill,
Looks round and murmurs, then again is still.

Now bring the remnants of each household fire;
On the wet ground the hissing coals expire;
And Paudeen Dhu, with meekly dismal face,
Receives the full possession of the place …

Whereon the Sheriff, 'We have legal hold.
Return to shelter with the sick and old.
Time shall be given; and there are carts below
If any to the workhouse choose to go.'
A young man makes him answer, grave and clear,
'We're thankful to you! but there's no one here
Goin' back into them houses: do your part.
Nor we won't trouble Pigot's horse and cart.'
At which name, rushing into th' open space,
A woman flings her hood from off her face,
Falls on her knees upon the miry ground,

Lifts hands and eyes, and voice of thrilling sound, —
'Vengeance of God Almighty fall on you,
James Pigot! — may the poor man's curse pursue,
The widow's and the orphan's curse, I pray,
Hang heavy round you at your dying day!'
Breathless and fix'd one moment stands the crowd
To hear this malediction fierce and loud.

But now (our neighbour Neal is busy there)
On steady poles he lifted Oona's chair,
Well-heap'd with borrow'd mantles; gently bear
The sick girl in her litter, bed and all;
Whilst others hug the children weak and small
In careful arms, or hoist them pick-a-back;
And, 'midst the unrelenting clink and thwack
Of iron bar on stone, let creep away
The sad procession from that hill-side grey,
Through the slow-falling rain. In three hours more
You find, where Ballytullagh stood before,
Mere shatter'd walls, and doors with useless latch,
And firesides buried under fallen thatch.

THE CELTS

Thomas D'Arcy McGee

Long, long ago, beyond the misty space
    Of twice a thousand years,
In Erin old there dwelt a mighty race,
    Taller than Roman spears;
Like oaks and towers they had a giant grace,
    Were fleet as deers,
With wind and waves they made their 'biding place,
    These western shepherd seers.

Their Ocean-God was Manannan MacLir,
    Whose angry lips,
In their white foam, full often would inter
    Whole fleets of ships;
Cromah their Day-God, and their Thunderer
    Made morning and eclipse;
Bride was their Queen of Song, and unto her
    They prayed with fire-touched lips.

Great were their deeds, their passions and their sports;
    With clay and stone
They piled on strath and shore those mystic forts,
    Not yet o'erthrown;
On cairn-crowned hills they held their council-courts;
    While youths alone,
With giant dogs, explored the elk resorts,
    And brought them down.

Stunts (c.1950)
Gerard Dillon (1916–1971)

Of these was Finn, the father of the Bard,
    Whose ancient song
Over the clamour of all change is heard,
    Sweet-voiced and strong.
Finn once o'ertook Grania, the golden-haired,
    The fleet and young;
From her the lovely, and from him the feared,
    The primal poet sprung.

Ossian! two thousand years of mist and change
    Surround thy name —
Thy Fenian heroes now no longer range
    The hills of fame.
The very names of Finn and Gaul sound strange —
    Yet thine the same —
By miscalled lake and desecrated grange —
    Remains, and shall remain!

The Druid's altar and the Druid's creed
    We scarce can trace,
There is not left an undisputed deed
    Of all your race,
Save your majestic song, which hath their speed,
    And strength and grace;
In that sole song, they live and love, and bleed —
    It bears them on through space.

O, inspired giant! shall we e'er behold,
    In our own time,
One fit to speak your spirit on the wold,
    Or seize your rhyme?
One pupil of the past, as mighty-souled
    As in the prime,
Were the fond, fair, and beautiful, and bold —
    They of your song sublime!

Celtic Twilight
Emmet McNamara (1976–)

FINNEGAN'S WAKE

Anon

Tim Finnegan lived in Walkin Street,
A gentleman Irish mighty odd,
He had a tongue both rich and sweet,
An' to rise in the world he carried a hod.
Now Tim had a sort of a tipplin' way,
With the love of the liquor he was born,
An' to help him on with his work each day;
He'd a drop of the craythur ev'ry morn.

Whack fol the dal, dance to your partner,
Welt the flure, yer trotters shake,
Wasn't it the truth I told you,
Lots of fun at Finnegan's Wake.

One morning Tim was rather full,
   His head felt heavy which make him shake,
He fell from the ladder and broke his skull,
   So they carried him home his corpse to wake,
They rolled him up in a nice clean sheet,
   And laid him out upon the bed,
With a gallon of whiskey at his feet,
   And a barrel of porter at his head.

His friends assembled at the wake,
   And Mrs Finnegan called for lunch,
First they brought in tay and cake,
   Then pipes, tobacco, and whiskey punch.
Miss Biddy O'Brien began to cry,
   'Such a neat clean corpse, did you ever see,
Arrah, Tim avouneen, why did you die?'
   'Ah, hould your gab,' said Paddy McGee.

Then Biddy O'Connor took up the job,
   'Biddy,' says she, 'you're wrong, I'm sure,'
But Biddy gave her a belt in the gob,
   And left her sprawling on the floor;
Oh, then the war did soon enrage;
   'Twas woman to woman and man to man,
Shillelagh law did all engage,
   And a row and a ruction soon began.

Then Micky Maloney raised his head,
   When a noggin of whiskey flew at him,
It missed and falling on the bed,
   The liquor scattered over Tim;
Bedad he revives, see how he rises,
   And Timothy rising from the bed,
Says, 'Whirl your liquor round like blazes,
   Thanam o'n dhoul, do ye think I'm dead!'

Figures Drinking
Mary Swanzy (1882–1978)

AFTER AUGHRIM

Hon. Emily Lawless

She said, 'They gave me of their best,
    They lived, they gave their lives for me;
I tossed them to the howling waste,
    And flung them to the foaming sea.'

She said, 'I never gave them aught,
    Not mine the power, if mine the will;
I let them starve, I let them bleed, —
    They bled and starved, and loved me still'.

She said, 'Ten times they fought for me,
    Ten times they strove with might and main,
Ten times I saw them beaten down,
    Ten times they rose, and fought again.'

She said, 'I stayed alone at home,
    A dreary woman, grey and cold;
I never asked them how they fared,
    Yet still they loved me as of old.'

She said, 'I never called them sons,
    I almost ceased to breathe their name,
Then caught it echoing down the wind,
    Blown backwards from the lips of Fame.'

She said, 'Not mine, not mine that fame;
    Far over sea, far over land,
Cast forth like rubbish from my shores,
    They won it yonder, sword in hand.'

She said, 'God knows they owe me naught,
    I tossed them to the foaming sea,
I tossed them to the howling waste,
    Yet still their love comes home to me.'

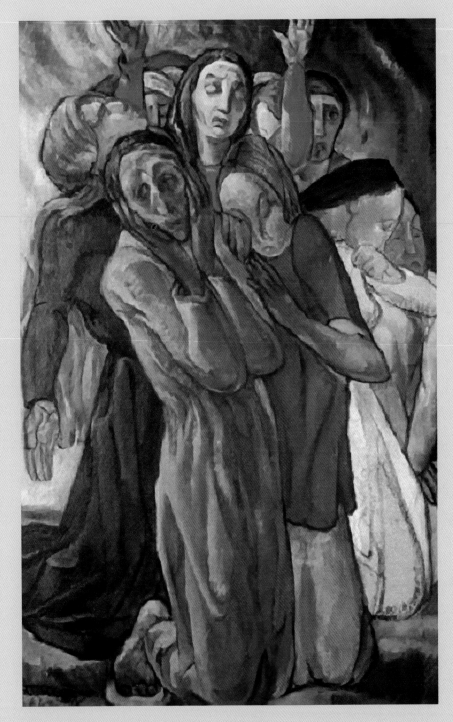

A Group of Sorrowing Women (1942)
Mary Swanzy (1882–1978)

THE MOUNTAINS OF MOURNE

Percy French

Oh, Mary, this London's a wonderful sight,

With people all working by day and by night.

Sure they don't sow potatoes, nor barley, nor wheat,

But there's gangs of them digging for gold in the street.

At least when I asked them that's what I was told,

So I just took a hand at this digging for gold,

But for all that I found there I might as well be

Where the Mountains of Mourne sweep down to the sea.

I believe that when writing a wish you expressed

As to know how the fine ladies in London were dressed;

Well if you'll believe me, when asked to a ball,

They don't wear no top to their dresses at all,

Oh I've seen them meself and you could not in truth,

Say that if they were bound for a ball or a bath.

Don't be starting such fashions, now, Mary mo chroi,

Where the Mountains of Mourne sweep down to the sea.

I've seen England's king from the top of a bus,

And I've never known him, but he means to know us.

And tho' by the Saxon we once were oppressed,

Still I cheered, God forgive me, I cheered with the rest.

And now that he's visited Erin's green shore

We'll be much better friends than we've been heretofore.

When we've got all we want, we're as quiet as can be

Where the mountains of Mourne sweep down to the sea.

Foothills of the Mournes
Arthur Campbell (1909–1994)

You remember young Peter O'Loughlin, of course,

Well, now he is here at the head of the force.

I met him today, I was crossing the Strand,

And he stopped the whole street with a wave of his hand.

And there we stood talkin' of days that are gone,

While the whole population of London looked on.

But for all these great powers he's wishful like me,

To be back where the dark Mourne sweeps down to the sea.

There's beautiful girls here, oh never you mind,

With beautiful shapes nature never designed,

And lovely complexions all roses and cream.

But let me remark with regard to the same:

That if of those roses you venture to sip,

The colours might all come away on your lip,

So I'll wait for the wild rose that's waiting for me

In the place where the dark Mourne sweeps down to the sea.

Mourne Mountains from Minerstown, Co. Down
Maurice Canning Wilks (1910–1984)

REQUIESCAT

Oscar Wilde

Tread lightly, she is near
   Under the snow,
Speak gently, she can hear
   The daisies grow.

All her bright golden hair
   Tarnished with rust,
She that was young and fair
   Fallen to dust.

Lily-like, white as snow,
   She hardly knew
She was a woman, so
   Sweetly she grew.

Coffin-board, heavy stone
   Lie on her breast,
I vex my heart alone,
   She is at rest.

Peace, Peace, she cannot hear
   Lyre or sonnet,
All my life's buried here,
   Heap earth upon it.

Sunday Morning
Frederick William Burton (1816–1900)

from THE BALLAD OF READING GAOL

Oscar Wilde

He did not wear his scarlet coat,
    For blood and wine are red,
And blood and wine were on his hands
    When they found him with the dead,
The poor dead woman whom he loved,
    And murdered in her bed.

He walked amongst the Trial Men
    In a suit of shabby gray;
A cricket cap was on his head,
    And his steps seemed light and gay;
But I never saw a man who looked
    So wistfully at the day.

★ ★ ★

I never saw a man who looked
    With such a wistful eye
Upon that little tent of blue
    Which prisoners call the sky,
And at every drifting cloud that went
    With sails of silver by.

I walked, with other souls in pain,
    Within another ring,
And was wondering if the man had done
    A great or little thing,
When a voice behind me whispered low,
    'That fellow's got to swing.'

Dear Christ! the very prison walls
    Suddenly seemed to reel,
And the sky above my head became
    Like a casque of scorching steel;
And, though I was a soul in pain,
    My pain I could not feel.

I only knew what hunted thought
    Quickened his step, and why
He looked upon the garish day
    With such a wistful eye;
The man had killed the thing he loved,
    And so he had to die.

Yet each man kills the thing he loves,
    By each let this be heard,
Some do it with a bitter look,
    Some with a flattering word,
The coward does it with a kiss,
    The brave man with a sword!

Some kill their love when they are young,
    And some when they are old;
Some strangle with the hands of Lust,
    Some with the hands of Gold:
The kindest use a knife, because
    The dead so soon grow cold.

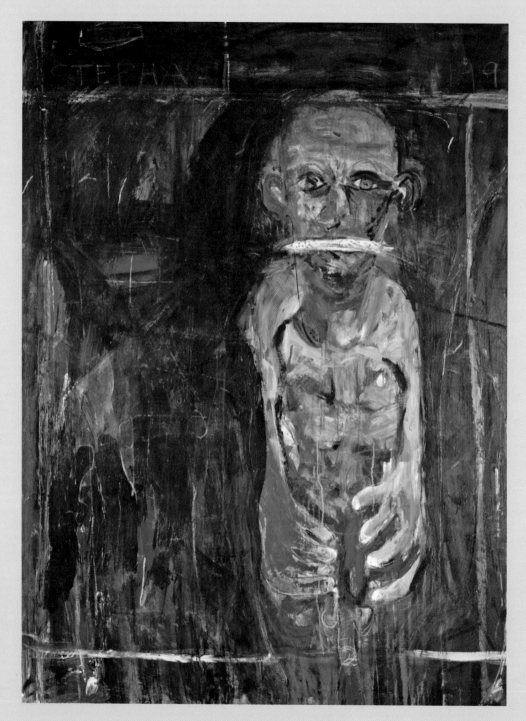

Figure Silenced (1991)
Brian Maguire (1951–)

Some love too little, some too long,
  Some sell, and others buy;
Some do the deed with many tears,
  And some without a sigh:
For each man kills the thing he loves,
  Yet each man does not die.

★ ★ ★

He does not die a death of shame
  On a day of dark disgrace,
Nor have a noose about his neck,
  Nor a cloth upon his face,
Nor drop feet foremost through the floor
  Into an empty place.

He does not sit with silent men
  Who watch him night and day;
Who watch him when he tries to weep,
  And when he tries to pray;
Who watch him lest himself should rob
  The prison of its prey.

He does not wake at dawn to see
  Dread figures throng his room,
The shivering Chaplain robed in white,
  The Sheriff stern with gloom,
And the Governor all in shiny black,
  With the yellow face of Doom.

He does not rise in piteous haste
  To put on convict-clothes,
While some coarse-mouthed Doctor gloats, and notes
  Each new and nerve-twitched pose,
Fingering a watch whose little ticks
  Are like horrible hammer-blows.

He does not know that sickening thirst
  That sands one's throat, before
The hangman with his gardener's gloves
  Slips through the padded door,
And binds one with three leathern thongs,
  That the throat may thirst no more.

He does not bend his head to hear
  The Burial Office read,
Nor, while the terror of his soul
  Tells him he is not dead,
Cross his own coffin, as he moves
  Into the hideous shed.

He does not stare upon the air
  Through a little roof of glass:
He does not pray with lips of clay
  For his agony to pass;
Nor feel upon his shuddering cheek
  The kiss of Caiaphas.

THE MAKING OF BIRDS

Katharine Tynan

God made Him birds in a pleasant humour;
    Tired of planets and suns was He.
He said: 'I will add a glory to Summer,
    Gifts for my creatures banished from Me!'

He had a thought and it set Him smiling
    Of the shape of a bird and its glancing head,
Its dainty air and its grace beguiling:
    'I will make feathers,' the Lord God said.

He made the robin; He made the swallow;
    His deft hands moulding the shape to His mood,
The thrush and lark and the finch to follow,
    And laughed to see that His work was good.

He Who has given men gift of laughter —
    Made in His image; He fashioned fit
The blink of the owl and the stork thereafter,
    The little wren and the long-tailed tit.

He spent in the making His wit and fancies;
    The wing-feathers He fashioned them strong;
Deft and dear as daisies and pansies,
    He crowned His work with the gift of song.

'Dearlings', He said, 'make songs for My praises!'
    He tossed them loose to the sun and wind,
Airily sweet as pansies and daisies;
    He taught them to build a nest to their mind.

The dear Lord God of His glories weary —
    Christ our Lord had the heart of a boy —
Made Him birds in a moment merry,
    Bade them soar and sing for His joy.

Feathered Pets
Francis Sylvester Walker (1848–1916)

The Bird Set Free
Beatrice Glenavy (1881–1970)

WHEN I WAS A LITTLE GIRL

Alice Milligan

When I was a little girl,
    In a garden playing
A thing was often said
    To chide us delaying:

When after sunny hours,
    At twilight's falling,
Down through the garden walks
    Came our old nurse calling.

'Come in! for it's growing late,
    And the grass will wet ye!
Come in! or when it's dark
    The Fenians will get ye.'

Then, at this dreadful news,
    All helter-skelter,
The panic-struck little flock
    Ran home for shelter.

And round the nursery fire
    Sat still to listen,
Fifty bare toes on the hearth,
    Ten eyes a-glisten.

To hear of a night in March,
    And loyal folk waiting,
To see a great army of men
    Come devastating.

An Army of Papists grim,
    With a green flag o'er them,
Red-coats and black police
    Flying before them.

But God (Who our nurse declared
    Guards British dominions)
Sent down a fall of snow
And scattered the Fenians.

'But somewhere they're lurking yet,
    Maybe they're near us,'
Four little hearts pit-a-pat
    Thought 'Can they hear us?'

Then the wind-shaken pane
    Sounded like drumming;
'Oh!' they cried, 'tuck us in,
    The Fenians are coming!'

Four little pairs of hands
In the cots where she led those,
Over their frightened heads
Pulled up the bedclothes.

But one little rebel there,
Watching all with laughter,
Thought, 'When the Fenians come
I'll rise and go after.'

Wished she had been a boy
And a good deal older —
Able to walk for miles
With a gun on her shoulder.

Able to lift aloft
The Green Flag o'er them
(Red-coats and black police
Flying before them).

And, as she dropped asleep,
Was wondering whether
God, if they prayed to Him,
Would give fine weather.

Children at the Barn
Erskine Nicol (1825–1904)

Red Hanrahan's Song about Ireland

W. B. Yeats

The old brown thorn-trees break in two high over Cummen Strand,

Under a bitter black wind that blows from the left hand;

Our courage breaks like an old tree in a black wind and dies,

But we have hidden in our hearts the flame out of the eyes

Of Cathleen, the daughter of Houlihan.

The wind has bundled up the clouds high over Knocknarea,

And thrown the thunder on the stones for all that Maeve can say.

Angers that are like noisy clouds have set our hearts abeat;

But we have all bent low and low and kissed the quiet feet

Of Cathleen, the daughter of Houlihan.

The yellow pool has overflowed high up on Clooth-na-Bare,

For the wet winds are blowing out of the clinging air;

Like heavy flooded waters our bodies and our blood;

But purer than a tall candle before the Holy Rood

Is Cathleen, the daughter of Houlihan.

Farmland Path
William Percy French (1854–1920)

EASTER, 1916

W. B. Yeats

I have met them at close of day
Coming with vivid faces
From counter or desk among grey
Eighteenth-century houses.
I have passed with a nod of the head
Or polite meaningless words,
Or have lingered awhile and said
Polite meaningless words,
And thought before I had done
Of a mocking tale or a gibe
To please a companion
Around the fire at the club,
Being certain that they and I
But lived where motley is worn:
All changed, changed utterly:
A terrible beauty is born.

That woman's days were spent
In ignorant good-will,
Her nights in argument
Until her voice grew shrill.
What voice more sweet than hers
When, young and beautiful,
She rode to harriers?
This man had kept a school
And rode our wingèd horse;
This other his helper and friend
Was coming into his force;
He might have won fame in the end,
So sensitive his nature seemed,
So daring and sweet his thought.
This other man I had dreamed
A drunken, vainglorious lout.
He had done most bitter wrong
To some who are near my heart,
Yet I number him in the song;
He, too, has resigned his part
In the casual comedy;
He, too, has been changed in his turn,
Transformed utterly:
A terrible beauty is born.

The Breadline (1916)
Muriel Brandt (1909–1981)

Hearts with one purpose alone
Through summer and winter seem
Enchanted to a stone
To trouble the living stream.
The horse that comes from the road,
The rider, the birds that range
From cloud to tumbling cloud,
Minute by minute they change;
A shadow of cloud on the stream
Changes minute by minute;
A horse-hoof slides on the brim,
And a horse plashes within it;
The long-legged moor-hens dive,
And hens to moor-cocks call;
Minute by minute they live:
The stone's in the midst of all.

Too long a sacrifice
Can make a stone of the heart.
O when may it suffice?
That is Heaven's part, our part
To murmur name upon name,
As a mother names her child
When sleep at last has come
On limbs that had run wild.
What is it but nightfall?
No, no, not night but death;
Was it needless death after all?
For England may keep faith
For all that is done and said.
We know their dream; enough
To know they dreamed and are dead;
And what if excess of love
Bewildered them till they died?
I write it out in a verse –
MacDonagh and MacBride
And Connolly and Pearse
Now and in time to be,
Wherever green is worn,
Are changed, changed utterly:
A terrible beauty is born.

A Prayer for my Daughter

W. B. Yeats

Once more the storm is howling, and half hid
Under this cradle-hood and coverlid
My child sleeps on. There is no obstacle
But Gregory's wood and one bare hill
Whereby the haystack- and roof-levelling wind,
Bred on the Atlantic, can be stayed;
And for an hour I have walked and prayed
Because of the great gloom that is in my mind.

I have walked and prayed for this young child an hour
And heard the sea-wind scream upon the tower,
And under the arches of the bridge, and scream
In the elms above the flooded stream;
Imagining in excited reverie
That the future years had come,
Dancing to a frenzied drum,
Out of the murderous innocence of the sea.

May she be granted beauty and yet not
Beauty to make a stranger's eye distraught,
Or hers before a looking-glass, for such,
Being made beautiful overmuch,
Consider beauty a sufficient end,
Lose natural kindness and maybe
The heart-revealing intimacy
That chooses right, and never find a friend.

Helen being chosen found life flat and dull
And later had much trouble from a fool,
While that great Queen, that rose out of the spray,
Being fatherless could have her way
Yet chose a bandy-leggèd smith for man.
It's certain that fine women eat
A crazy salad with their meat
Whereby the Horn of Plenty is undone.

In courtesy I'd have her chiefly learned;
Hearts are not had as a gift but hearts are earned
By those that are not entirely beautiful;
Yet many, that have played the fool
For beauty's very self, has charm made wise,
And many a poor man that has roved,
Loved and thought himself beloved,
From a glad kindness cannot take his eyes.

May she become a flourishing hidden tree
That all her thoughts may like the linnet be,
And have no business but dispensing round
Their magnanimities of sound,
Nor but in merriment begin a chase,
Nor but in merriment a quarrel.
O may she live like some green laurel
Rooted in one dear perpetual place.

Mallaranny (1918–19)
Grace Henry (1863–1953)

My mind, because the minds that I have loved,
The sort of beauty that I have approved,
Prosper but little, has dried up of late,
Yet knows that to be choked with hate
May well be of all evil chances chief.
If there's no hatred in a mind
Assault and battery of the wind
Can never tear the linnet from the leaf.

An intellectual hatred is the worst,
So let her think opinions are accursed.
Have I not seen the loveliest woman born
Out of the mouth of Plenty's horn,
Because of her opinionated mind
Barter that horn and every good
By quiet natures understood
For an old bellows full of angry wind?

Considering that, all hatred driven hence,
The soul recovers radical innocence
And learns at last that it is self-delighting,
Self-appeasing, self-affrighting,
And that its own sweet will is Heaven's will;
She can, though every face should scowl
And every windy quarter howl
Or every bellows burst, be happy still.

And may her bridegroom bring her to a house
Where all's accustomed, ceremonious;
For arrogance and hatred are the wares
Peddled in the thoroughfares.
How but in custom and in ceremony
Are innocence and beauty born?
Ceremony's a name for the rich horn,
And custom for the spreading laurel tree.

THE STARE'S NEST BY MY WINDOW

W. B. Yeats

The bees build in the crevices
Of loosening masonry, and there
The mother birds bring grubs and flies.
My wall is loosening; honey-bees,
Come build in the empty house of the stare.

We are closed in, and the key is turned
On our uncertainty; somewhere
A man is killed, or a house burned,
Yet no clear fact to be discerned:
Come build in the empty house of the stare.

A barricade of stone or of wood;
Some fourteen days of civil war;
Last night they trundled down the road
That dead young soldier in his blood:
Come build in the empty house of the stare.

We had fed the heart on fantasies,
The heart's grown brutal from the fare;
More substance in our enmities
Than in our love; O honey-bees,
Come build in the empty house of the stare.

An Allegory (1922)
Sean Keating (1889–1977)

THE LOVE-TALKER

Ethna Carbery

I met the Love-Talker one eve in the glen,
He was handsomer than any of our handsome young men,
His eyes were blacker than the sloe, his voice sweeter far
Than the crooning of old Kevin's pipes beyond in Coolnagar.

I was bound for the milking with a heart fair and free —
My grief! my grief! that bitter hour drained the life from me;
I thought him human lover, though his lips on mine were cold,
And the breath of death blew keen on me within his hold.

I know not what way he came, no shadow fell behind,
But all the sighing rushes swayed beneath a fairy wind;
The thrush ceased its singing, a mist crept about,
We two clung together — with the world shut out.

Coortin' (c. 1922)
William Conor (1881–1968)

Beyond the ghostly mist I could hear my cattle low,

The little cow from Ballina, clean as driven snow,

The dun cow from Kerry, the roan from Inisheer,

Oh, pitiful their calling — and his whispers in my ear!

His eyes were a fire; his words were a snare;

I cried my mother's name, but no help was there;

I made the blessed Sign — then he gave a dreary moan,

A wisp of cloud went floating by, and I stood alone.

Running ever thro' my head is an old-time rune —

'Who meets the Love-Talker must weave her shroud soon.'

My mother's face is furrowed with the salt tears that fall,

But the kind eyes of my father are the saddest sight of all.

I have spun the fleecy lint and now my wheel is still,

The linen length is woven for my shroud fine and chill,

I shall stretch me on the bed where a happy maid I lay —

Pray for the soul of Máire Óg at dawning of the day!

Stepping Out Together
William Conor (1881–1968)

GERMINAL

George 'AE' Russell

Call not thy wanderer home as yet
    Though it be late.
Now is his first assailing of
    The invisible gate.
Be still through that light knocking. The hour
    Is thronged with fate.

To that first tapping at the invisible door
    Fate answereth.
What shining image or voice, what sigh
    Or honied breath,
Comes forth, shall be the master of life
    Even to death.

Satyrs may follow after. Seraphs
    On crystal wing
May blaze. But the delicate first-comer
    It shall be King.
They shall obey, even the mightiest,
    That gentle thing.

All the strong powers of Dante were bowed
    To a child's mild eyes,
That wrought within him that travail
    From depths up to skies,
Inferno, Purgatorio
    And Paradise.

Amid the soul's grave councillors
    A petulant boy
Laughs under the laurels and purples, the elf
    Who snatched at his joy,
Ordering Caesar's legions to bring him
    The world for his toy.

In ancient shadows and twilights
    Where childhood had strayed,
The world's great sorrows were born
    And its heroes were made.
In the lost boyhood of Judas
    Christ was betrayed.

Let thy young wanderer dream on:
    Call him not home.
A door opens, a breath, a voice
    From the ancient room,
Speaks to him now. Be it dark or bright
    He is knit with his doom.

The Meeting of St Brendan with the Unhappy Judas (1911)
Harry Clarke (1889–1931)

QUEENS
J.M. Synge

Seven dog-days we let pass
Naming Queens in Glenmacnass,
All the rare and royal names
Wormy sheepskin yet retains,
Etain, Helen, Maeve, and Fand,
Golden Deirdre's tender hand,
Bert, the big-foot, sung by Villon,
Cassandra, Ronsard found in Lyon.
Queens of Sheba, Meath and Connaught,
Coifed with crown, or gaudy bonnet,
Queens whose finger once did stir men,
Queens were eaten of fleas and vermin,
Queens men drew like Mona Lisa,
Or slew with drugs in Rome and Pisa,

We named Lucrezia Crivelli,
And Titian's lady with amber belly,
Queens acquainted in learned sin,
Jane of Jewry's slender shin:
Queens who cut the bogs of Glanna,
Judith of Scripture, and Gloriana,
Queens who wasted the East by proxy,
Or drove the ass-cart, a tinker's doxy,
Yet these are rotten – I ask their pardon –
And we've the sun on rock and garden,
These are rotten, so you're the Queen
Of all are living, or have been.

Ligeia
Harry Clarke (1889–1931)

THE MEMORY

Lord Dunsany

I watch the doctors walking with the nurses to and fro

And I hear them softly talking in the garden where they go,

But I envy not their learning, nor their right of walking free,

For the emperor of Tartary has died for love of me.

I can see his face all golden beneath his night-black hair,

And the temples strange and olden in the gleaming eastern air,

Where he walked alone and sighing because I would not sail

To the lands where he was dying for a love of no avail.

He had seen my face by magic in a mirror that they make

For those rulers proud and tragic by their lotus-covered lake,

Where there hangs a pale-blue tiling on an alabaster wall.

And he loved my way of smiling, and loved nothing else at all.

There were peacocks there and peaches, and green monuments of jade,

Where macaws with sudden screeches made the little dogs afraid,

And the silver fountains sprinkled foreign flowers on the sward

As they rose and curved and tinkled for their listless yellow lord.

Ah well, he's dead and rotten in his far magnolia grove,

But his love is unforgotten and I need no other love,

And with open eyes when sleeping, or closed eyes when awake,

I can see the fountains leaping by the borders of the lake.

They call it my delusion; they may call it what they will,

For the times are in confusion and are growing wilder still,

And there are no splendid memories in any face I see.

But an emperor of Tartary has died for love of me.

The Mad Woman of Douai (1918)
William Orpen (1878–1931)

RINGSEND

Oliver St John Gogarty

I will live in Ringsend
With a red-headed whore,
And the fan-light gone in
Where it lights the hall-door;
And listen each night
For her querulous shout,
As at last she streels in
And the pubs empty out.
To soothe that wild breast
With my old-fangled songs,
Till she feels it redressed
From inordinate wrongs,
Imagined, outrageous,
Preposterous wrongs,
Till peace at last comes,
Shall be all I will do,
Where the little lamp blooms
Like a rose in the stew;
And up the back-garden
The sound comes to me
Of the lapsing, unsoilable,
Whispering sea.

Murphy's Boat-Yard, Ringsend, Dublin (1940)
Harry Kernoff (1900–1974)

THE LAMPLIGHTER
Seumas O'Sullivan

Here to the leisured side of life,
Remote from traffic, free from strife,
A cul-de-sac, a sanctuary
Where old quaint customs creep to die
And only ancient memories stir,
At evening comes the lamplighter;
With measured steps, without a sound,
He treads the unalterable round,
Soundlessly touching one by one
The waiting posts that stand to take
The faint blue bubbles in his wake;
And when the night begins to wane
He comes to take them back again,
Before the chilly dawn can blight
The delicate frail buds of light.

Lamplight
Tom Kerr (1925–)

BLANAID'S SONG

Joseph Campbell

Blanaid loves roses;
And Lugh who disposes
All beautiful things,
Gave her
      Roses.

All heavenly things,
Dreambegot, fairyborn,
All natural things
Of colour and savour:
(Shawls of old kings,
Ripeness of corn,
Butterfly wings,
Veined chestnut leaves,
Dark summer eves,
Moons at high morn).
He searched for a favour,
And, pondering, gave her
      Roses.

Blanaid's black head
Wears a barret of red
From Lugh's gardenlands;
Her breasts and her hands
Are burthened with
      Roses.

— So her song closes!

Roses at Kilmurray
Mildred Anne Butler (1858–1941)

SCENE-SHIFTER DEATH

Mary Devenport O'Neill

As it is true that I, like all, must die,
I crave that death may take me unawares
At the very end of some transcendent day;
May creep upon me when I least suspect,
And, with slick fingers light as feather tips,
Unfasten every little tenuous bolt
That held me all my years to this illusion
Of flesh and blood and air and land and sea.

I'd have death work meticulously too —
Splitting each moment into tenths of tenths
Replacing each infinitesimal fragment
Of old dream-stuff with new.

So subtly will the old be shed
That I'll dream on and never know I'm dead.

Time Flies
William Gerard Barry (1864–1941)

SHE MOVED THROUGH THE FAIR

Padraic Colum

My young love said to me,
My mother won't mind
And my father won't slight you
For your lack of kind.
And she laid her hand on me
And this she did say:
It will not be long, love,
'Til our wedding day.

As she stepped away from me
And she moved through the fair,
And fondly I watched her
Move here and move there.
And then she turned homeward,
With one star awake,
Like the swan in the evening
Moves over the lake.

The people were saying,
No two e'er were wed
But one had a sorrow
That never was said.
And I smiled as she passed
With her goods and her gear,
And that was the last
That I saw of my dear.

Last night she came to me,
My dead love came in.
So softly she came
That her feet made no din.
As she laid her hand on me,
And this she did say:
It will not be long, love,
'Til our wedding day.

A Fair
Francis Sylvester Walker (1848–1916)

The Bride
Daniel O'Neill (1920–1974)

A Dublin Ballad – 1916

Dermot O'Byrne (Arnold Bax)

O write it up above your hearth
And troll it out to sun and moon,
To all true Irishmen on earth
Arrest and death come late or soon.

Some boy-o whistled *Ninety-eight*
One Sunday night in College Green,
And such a broth of love and hate
Was stirred ere Monday morn was late
As Dublin town had never seen.

And god-like forces shocked and shook
Through Irish hearts that lively day,
And hope it seemed no ill could brook.
Christ! for that liberty they took
There was the ancient deuce to pay!

The deuce in all his bravery,
His girth and gall grown no whit less,
He swarmed in from the fatal sea
With pomp of huge artillery
And brass and copper haughtiness.

He cracked up all the town with guns
That roared loud psalms to fire and death,
And houses hailed down granite tons
To smash our wounded underneath.

And when at last the golden bell
Of liberty was silenced — then
He learned to shoot extremely well
At unarmed Irish gentlemen!

Ah! where were Michael and gold Moll
And Seumas and my drowsy self?
Why did fate blot us from the scroll?
Why were we left upon the shelf,

Fooling with trifles in the dark
When the light struck so wild and hard?
Sure our hearts were as good a mark
For Tommies up before the lark
At rifle practice in the yard!

Well, the last fire is trodden down,
Our dead are rotting fast in lime,
We all can sneak back into town,
Stravague about as in old time,

And stare at gaps of grey and blue
Where Lower Mount Street used to be,
And where flies hum round muck we knew
For Abbey Street and Eden Quay.

And when the devil's made us wise
Each in his own peculiar hell,
With desert hearts and drunken eyes
We're free to sentimentalize
By corners where the martyrs fell.

British Soldiers in Dublin (1916)
Lilian Lucy Davidson (1893–1954)

JUNE

Francis Ledwidge

Broom out the floor now, lay the fender by,

And plant this bee-sucked bough of woodbine there,

And let the window down. The butterfly

Floats in upon the sunbeam, and the fair

Tanned face of June, the nomad gipsy, laughs

Above her widespread wares, the while she tells

The farmers' fortunes in the fields, and quaffs

The water from the spider-peopled wells.

Collecting Flowers
Mildred Anne Butler (1858–1941)

The hedges are all drowned in green grass seas,
And bobbing poppies flare like Elmo's light,
While siren-like the pollen-stainèd bees
Drone in the clover depths. And up the height
The cuckoo's voice is hoarse and broke with joy.
And on the lowland crops the crows make raid,
Nor fear the clappers of the farmer's boy,
Who sleeps, like drunken Noah, in the shade.

And loop this red rose in that hazel ring
That snares your little ear, for June is short
And we must joy in it and dance and sing,
And from her bounty draw her rosy worth.
Ay! soon the swallows will be flying south,
The wind wheel north to gather in the snow,
Even the roses spilt on youth's red mouth
Will soon blow down the road all roses go.

August Landscape, Boa Island (c.1969)
Colin Middleton (1910–1983)

UNMARRIED MOTHERS

Austin Clarke

In the Convent of the Sacred Heart,

The Long Room has been decorated

Where a Bishop can dine off golden plate:

As Oriental Potentate.

Girls, who will never wheel a go-cart,

Cook, sew, wash, dig, milk cows, clean stables

And, twice a day, giving their babes

The teat, herdlike, yield milk that cost

Them dearly, when their skirts were tossed up

Above their haunches. Hook or zip

Has warded them at Castlepollard.

Luckier girls, on board a ship,

Watch new hope springing from the bollard.

Women and Children
George 'AE' Russell (1867–1935)

THE PLANTER'S DAUGHTER

Austin Clarke

When night stirred at sea
And the fire brought a crowd in,
They say that her beauty
Was music in mouth
And few in the candlelight
Thought her too proud,
For the house of the planter
Is known by the trees.

Men that had seen her
Drank deep and were silent,
The women were speaking
Wherever she went –
As a bell that is rung
Or a wonder told shyly,
And O she was the Sunday
In every week.

Girl in White
Sarah Purser (1848–1943)

SONG FOR THE CLATTER-BONES

F.R. Higgins

God rest that Jewy woman,

Queen Jezebel, the bitch

Who peeled the clothes from her shoulder-bones

Down to her spent teats

As she stretched out of the window

Among the geraniums, where

She chaffed and laughed like one half daft

Titivating her painted hair —

King Jehu he drove to her,

She tipped him a fancy beck;

But he from his knacky side-car spoke,

'Who'll break that dewlapped neck?'

And so she was thrown from the window;

Like Lucifer she fell

Beneath the feet of the horses and they beat

The light out of Jezebel.

That corpse wasn't planted in clover;

Ah, nothing of her was found

Save those grey bones that Hare-foot Mike

Gave me for their lovely sound;

And as once her dancing body

Made star-lit princes sweat,

So I'll just clack: though her ghost lacks a back

There's music in the old bones yet.

Show Me the Way to the Lollipop Kids
Charlotte Mangan (1978–)

DIAMOND CUT DIAMOND

Ewart Milne

Two cats

One up a tree

One under the tree

The cat up a tree is he

The cat under the tree is she

The tree is witch elm, just incidentally.

He takes no notice of she, she takes no notice of he.

He stares at the woolly clouds passing, she stares at the tree.

There's been a lot written about cats, by Old Possum, Yeats, and Company,

But not Alfred de Musset or Lord Tennyson or Poe or anybody

Wrote about one cat under, and one cat up, a tree.

God knows why this should be left for me

Except I like cats as cats be

Especially one cat up

And one cat under

A witch elm

Tree.

Yellow Bungalow
Gerard Dillon (1916–1971)

TO BE DEAD

Patrick Kavanagh

To be dead is to stop believing in
The masterpieces we will begin tomorrow;
To be an exile is to be a coward,
To know that growth has stopped,
That whatever is done is the end;
Correct the proofs over and over,
Rewrite old poems again and again,
Tell lies to yourself about your achievement:
Ten printed books on the shelves.
Though you know that no one loves you for
what you have done,
But for what you might do.

And you perhaps, take up religion bitterly
Which you laughed at in your youth,
Well not actually laughed
But it wasn't your kind of truth.

An Island Funeral (1923)
Jack Butler Yeats (1871–1957)

SHANCODUFF

Patrick Kavanagh

My black hills have never seen the sun rising,
Eternally they look north towards Armagh.
Lot's wife would not be salt if she had been
Incurious as my black hills that are happy
When dawn whitens Glassdrummond chapel.

My hills hoard the bright shillings of March
While the sun searches in every pocket.
They are my Alps and I have climbed the Matterhorn
With a sheaf of hay for three perishing calves
In the field under the Big Forth of Rocksavage.

The sleety winds fondle the rushy beards of Shancoduff
While the cattle-drovers sheltering in the Featherna Bush
Look up and say: 'Who owns them hungry hills
That the water-hen and snipe must have forsaken?
A poet? Then by heavens he must be poor'
I hear and is my heart not badly shaken?

Morning Mountain, Connemara (1944)
Louis le Brocquy (1916–)
(watercolour, 14 × 25 cm)

from LOUGH DERG

Patrick Kavanagh

From Cavan and from Leitrim and from Mayo,
From all the thin-faced parishes where hills
Are perished noses running peaty water,
They come to Lough Derg to fast and pray and beg
With all the bitterness of nonentities, and the envy
Of the inarticulate when dealing with an artist.
Their hands push closed the doors that God holds open.
Love-sunlit is an enchanter in June's hours
And flowers and light. These to shopkeepers and small lawyers
Are heresies up beauty's sleeve.

The naïve and simple go on pilgrimage too,
Lovers trying to take God's truth for granted …
Listen to the chanted
Evening devotions in the limestone church,
For this is Lough Derg, St Patrick's Purgatory.
He came to this island-acre of greenstone once
To be shut of the smug too-faithful. The story
Is different now:
Solicitors praying for cushy jobs,
To be County Registrar or Coroner;
Shopkeepers threatened with sharper rivals
Than any hook-nosed foreigner;
Mothers whose daughters are Final Medicals,
Too heavy-hipped for thinking;
Wives whose husbands have angina pectoris,
Wives whose husbands have taken to drinking.

But there were the sincere as well,

The innocent who feared the hell

Of sin. The girl who had won

A lover and the girl who had none

Were both in trouble,

Trying to encave in the rubble

Of these rocks the Real,

The part that can feel.

And the half-pilgrims too,

They who are the true

Spirit of Ireland, who joke

Through the Death-mask and take

Virgins of heaven or flesh,

Were on Lough Derg Island

Wanting some half-wish.

Mass in a Connemara Cabin
Aloysius O'Kelly (1853–*c.*1941)

Over the black waves of the lake trip the last echoes

Of the bell that has shooed through the chapel door

The last pilgrims, like hens to roost.

The sun through Fermanagh's furze fingers

Looks now on the deserted penance rings of stone

Where only John Flood on St Kevin's Bed lingers

With the sexton's heaven-sure stance, the man who knows

The ins and outs of religion …

'Hail glorious St Patrick' a girl sings above

The old-man drone of the harmonium.

The rosary is said and Benediction.

The Sacramental sun turns round and 'Holy, Holy, Holy'

The pilgrims cry, striking their breasts in Purgatory.

The same routine and ritual now

As serves for street processions or Congresses

That take all shapes of souls as a living theme

In a novel refuses nothing. No truth oppresses.

Children Playing at a Crossroads (c.*1838*)
Trevor Fowler (1800–*c*.1844)

Women and men in bare feet turn again

To the iron crosses and the rutted Beds,

Their feet are swollen and their bellies empty —

But something that is Ireland's secret leads

These petty mean people,

For here's the day of a poor soul freed

To a marvellous beauty above its head.

The Castleblayney grocer trapped in the moment's need

Puts out a hand and writes what he cannot read,

A wisdom astonished at every turn

By some angel that writes in the oddest words.

When he will walk again in Muckno Street

He'll hear from the kitchens of fair-day eating houses

In the after-bargain carouses

News from a country beyond the range of birds.

ONCE ALIEN HERE

John Hewitt

Once alien here my fathers built their house,
claimed, drained, and gave the land the shapes of use,
and for their urgent labour grudged no more
than shuffled pennies from the hoarded store
of well rubbed words that had left their overtones
in the ripe England of the moulded downs.

The sullen Irish limping to the hills
bore with them the enchantments and the spells
that in the clans' free days hung gay and rich
on every twig of every thorny hedge,
and gave the rain-pocked stone a meaning past
the blurred engraving of the fibrous frost.

So I, because of all the buried men
in Ulster clay, because of rock and glen
and mist and cloud and quality of air
as native in my thought as any here,
who now would seek a native mode to tell
our stubborn wisdom individual,
yet lacking skill in either scale of song,
the graver English, lyric Irish tongue,
must let this rich earth so enhance the blood
with steady pulse where now is plunging mood
till thought and image may, identified,
find easy voice to utter each aright.

Autumn Landscape, Co. Down
Betty Christie (1952–)

DUBLIN
Louis MacNeice

Grey brick upon brick,
Declamatory bronze
On sombre pedestals —
O'Connell, Grattan, Moore —
And the brewery tugs and the swans
On the balustraded stream
And the bare bones of a fanlight
Over a hungry door
And the air soft on the cheek
And porter running from the taps
With a head of yellow cream
And Nelson on his pillar
Watching his world collapse.

This was never my town,
I was not born nor bred
Nor schooled here and she will not
Have me alive or dead
But yet she holds my mind
With her seedy elegance,
With her gentle veils of rain
And all her ghosts that walk
And all that hide behind
Her Georgian façades —
The catcalls and the pain,
The glamour of her squalor,
The bravado of her talk.

Nelson's Pillar, Sackville Street, Dublin (1832)
George Petrie (1790–1866)

The lights jig in the river
With a concertina movement
And the sun comes up in the morning
Like barley-sugar on the water
And the mist on the Wicklow hills
Is close, as close
As the peasantry were to the landlord,
As the Irish to the Anglo-Irish,
As the killer is close one moment
To the man he kills,
Or as the moment itself
Is close to the next moment.

She is not an Irish town
And she is not English,
Historic with guns and vermin
And the cold renown
Of a fragment of Church latin,
Of an oratorical phrase.
But O the days are soft,
Soft enough to forget
The lesson better learnt,
The bullet on the wet
Streets, the crooked deal,
The steel behind the laugh,
The Four Courts burnt.

Fort of the Dane,
Garrison of the Saxon,
Augustan capital
Of a Gaelic nation,
Appropriating all
The alien brought,
You give me time for thought
And by a juggler's trick
You poise the toppling hour —
O greyness run to flower,
Grey stone, grey water
And brick upon grey brick.

Sketch for the Funeral of Terence McSwiney,
Lord Mayor of Cork, 1920
John Lavery (1856–1941)

from AUTUMN JOURNAL

Louis MacNeice

XVI

Nightmare leaves fatigue:
    We envy men of action
Who sleep and wake, murder and intrigue
    Without being doubtful, without being haunted.
And I envy the intransigence of my own
    Countrymen who shoot to kill and never
See the victim's face become their own
    Or find his motive sabotage their motives.
So reading the memoirs of Maud Gonne,
    Daughter of an English mother and a soldier father,
I note how a single purpose can be founded on
    A jumble of opposites:
Dublin Castle, the vice-regal ball,
    The embassies of Europe,
Hatred scribbled on a wall,
    Gaols and revolvers.
And I remember, when I was little, the fear
    Bandied among the servants
That Casement would land at the pier
    With a sword and a horde of rebels;
And how we used to expect, at a later date,
    When the wind blew from the west, the noise of shooting
Starting in the evening at eight
    In Belfast in the York Street district;

Maude Gonne (1891)
Sarah Purser (1848–1943)

And the voodoo of the Orange bands
    Drawing an iron net through darkest Ulster,
Flailing the limbo lands –
    The linen mills, the long wet grass, the ragged hawthorn.
And one read black where the other read white, his hope
    The other man's damnation:
Up the Rebels, To Hell with the Pope,
    And God Save – as you prefer – the King or Ireland.
The land of scholars and saints:
    Scholars and saints my eye, the land of ambush,
Purblind manifestoes, never-ending complaints,
    The born martyr and the gallant ninny;
The grocer drunk with the drum,
    The land-owner shot in his bed, the angry voices
Piercing the broken fanlight in the slum,
    The shawled woman weeping at the garish altar.
Kathaleen ni Houlihan! Why
    Must a country, like a ship or a car, be always female,
Mother or sweetheart? A woman passing by,
    We did but see her passing.
Passing like a patch of sun on the rainy hill
    And yet we love her for ever and hate our neighbour
And each one in his will
    Binds his heirs to continuance of hatred.

College Green, Dublin
Rose Maynard Barton (1856–1929)

Still Life at my Window
George Campbell (1917–1979)

Drums on the haycock, drums on the harvest, black
    Drums in the night shaking the windows:
King William is riding his white horse back
    To the Boyne on a banner.
Thousands of banners, thousands of white
    Horses, thousands of Williams
Waving thousands of swords and ready to fight
    Till the blue sea turns to orange.
Such was my country and I thought I was well
    Out of it, educated and domiciled in England,
Though yet her name keeps ringing like a bell
    In an under-water belfry.
Why do we like being Irish? Partly because
    It gives us a hold on the sentimental English
As members of a world that never was,
    Baptised with fairy water;
And partly because Ireland is small enough
    To be still thought of with a family feeling,
And because the waves are rough
    That split her from a more commercial culture;
And because one feels that here at least one can
    Do local work which is not at the world's mercy
And that on this tiny stage with luck a man
    Might see the end of one particular action.

It is self-deception of course;

    There is no immunity in this island either;

A cart that is drawn by somebody else's horse

    And carrying goods to somebody else's market.

The bombs in the turnip sack, the sniper from the roof,

    Griffith, Connolly, Collins, where have they brought us?

Ourselves alone! Let the round tower stand aloof

    In a world of bursting mortar!

Let the school-children fumble their sums

    In a half-dead language;

Let the censor be busy on the books; pull down the Georgian slums;

    Let the games be played in Gaelic.

Let them grow beet-sugar; let them build

    A factory in every hamlet;

Let them pigeon-hole the souls of the killed

    Into sheep and goats, patriots and traitors.

And the North, where I was a boy,

    Is still the North, veneered with the grime of Glasgow,

Thousands of men whom nobody will employ

    Standing at the corners, coughing.

And the street-children play on the wet

    Pavement – hopscotch or marbles;

And each rich family boasts a sagging tennis-net

    On a spongy lawn beside a dripping shrubbery.

The Small Ring
Jack Butler Yeats (1871–1957)

Carrying Turf
Francis Sylvester Walker (1848–1916)

The smoking chimneys hint
     At prosperity round the corner
But they make their Ulster linen from foreign lint
     And the money that comes in goes out to make more money.
A city built upon mud;
     A culture built upon profit;
Free speech nipped in the bud,
     The minority always guilty.
Why should I want to go back
     To you, Ireland, my Ireland?
The blots on the page are so black
     That they cannot be covered with shamrock.
I hate your grandiose airs,
     Your sob-stuff, your laugh and your swagger,
Your assumption that everyone cares
     Who is the king of your castle.
Castles are out of date,
     The tide flows round the children's sandy fancy;
Put up what flag you like, it is too late
     To save your soul with bunting.
Odi atque amo:
     Shall we cut this name on trees with a rusty dagger?
Her mountains are still blue, her rivers flow
     Bubbling over the boulders.
She is both a bore and a bitch;
     Better close the horizon,
Send her no more fantasy, no more longings which
     Are under a fatal tariff.
For common sense is the vogue
     And she gives her children neither sense nor money
Who slouch around the world with a gesture and a brogue
     And a faggot of useless memories.

THE WORKMAN'S FRIEND
Flann O'Brien (Brian O'Nolan)

When things go wrong and will not come right,
Though you do the best you can,
When life looks black as the hour of night —
A pint of plain is your only man.

When money's tight and is hard to get,
And your horse has also ran,
When all you have is a heap of debt —
A pint of plain is your only man.

When health is bad and your heart feels strange,
And your face is pale and wan,
When doctors say that you need a change —
A pint of plain is your only man.

When food is scarce and your larder bare,
And no rashers grease your pan,
When hunger grows as your meals are rare —
A pint of plain is your only man.

In time of trouble and lousey strife,
You have still got a darlint plan,
You still can turn to a brighter life —
A pint of plain is your only man.

Jocose, Bellicose, Lachrymose (1973)
Sean Keating (1889–1977)

NOSTALGIE D'AUTOMNE
Leslie Daiken

Island of Shadow
Silk of the Kine
Mouse in the meadow
And crab-apple wine

Sun on the brambles
Rocking a pram
And driving the yellow
Wasps offa the jam

Sugar-pears hangin
Ripe ready to fall
And a lass stringin mushrooms
In warm Donegal

Starlings at sunset
Linnets at noon
And cat-owl and cricket
Cry out with the moon

Island of Shadow
Silk of the Kine
Will Sickle and Hammer
Ever be thine?

Melon and marrow
Stored by the load
Here on a barrow
In Theobald's Road.

In a Dublin Park (1898)
Walter Frederick Osborne (1859–1903)

THE JACKEEN'S LAMENT FOR THE BLASKETS

Brendan Behan

The sea will be under the sun like an empty mirror,
No boat under sail, no sign of a living sinner
And nothing reflected but one golden eagle, the last,
On the edge of the world beyond the lonely Blaskets.

The sun will be setting, the shadows of night dispersing
As the rising moon shines down through the sea-cold night cloud,
Her long, bare fingers stretched down to the empty earth
And the houses fallen and ruined and broken apart.

The only sounds the hush of the birds' soft feathers
Skimming over the water, returning safe and together,
And the wind as it sighs and softly swings the half-door
Mourning a hearth that is cold for ever more.

Translated by Donagh MacDonagh

High Sky Over The Blaskets
David Clarke (1920–2006)

BALLAD TO A TRADITIONAL REFRAIN

Maurice James Craig

Red brick in the suburbs, white horse on the wall,
Eyetalian marbles in the City Hall:
O stranger from England, why stand so aghast?
May the Lord in His mercy be kind to Belfast!

This jewel that houses our hopes and our fears
Was knocked up from the swamp in the last hundred years;
But the last shall be first and the first shall be last:
May the Lord in His mercy be kind to Belfast!

We swore by King William there'd never be seen
An all-Irish Parliament at College Green,
So at Stormont we're nailing the flag to the mast:
May the Lord in His mercy be kind to Belfast!

O the bricks they will bleed and the rain it will weep
And the damp Lagan fog lull the city to sleep;
It's to hell with the future and live on the past:
May the Lord in His mercy be kind to Belfast!

Twelfth Parade – North Queen Street (1991)
Joseph McWilliams (1938–)

THE GLORIOUS TWELFTH, 12 JULY 1943

Robert Greacen

You will remember that the Twelfth was always dry,
That rain followed the day after, some said as Judgement,
While others argued that drums of Ulster stirring
Pulled out the corded wetness from our local skies.
Four years ago we heard them last, heard the thunder
Smouldering through the ribboned streets towards the battle
In the fields of Finaghy. There was fire then,
Fire in our throats, fire beaten out from our cities,
Cold, distant, strongly arid in the normal weather:
Four years ago since last we heard the drums' thunder,
Since the Orange banners looped in gay procession
And bands of flute and fife, of brass and silver
Played hell to the Pope and immortality to William —
To William, Prince of Orange, defender and avenger,
To William, the stiff Dutch Protestant who saved us
From villainous James, the tyrant Stuart King.

Remember 1690, remember the ancient wrongs of Rome,
Remember Derry, Aughrim, Enniskillen and the Boyne,
The Glorious Boyne in Ireland, where the Pope was overcome,
Remember the Maiden City and the breaking of her boom.

The Orange Parade passing St Patricks Church
Joseph McWilliams (1938–)

These were my people marching on the streets,

Released from inhibition and resolved to keep the faith.

Four years have passed since Ulster opened up her heart,

And toasted her deliverance from the Seven Hills,

Four years since fire has run swift rivers into Europe

From Dunkirk to Briansk, from Naples to Novgorod,

From Caucasus to Clyde, from Warsaw to Belfast.

And now, in Derry and Downpatrick, no Ulstermen are marching

To the rustle of their banners and the flogging of their drums.

Our red-brick cities have their blackened skeletons,

Our people carry the public and the personal wound.

Forgotten 1690, forgotten the ancient wrongs of Rome,

Forgotten Derry, Aughrim, Enniskillen and the Boyne,

The Glorious Boyne in Ireland where the Pope was overcome,

Forgotten the Maiden City and the breaking of her boom.

You will remember that the Twelfth was always dry,

While now in Italy the bloods of Continents are joined,

While now the Russian plains are stacked with corpses,

Rotting in the Red sun, feeding plagues to common rats …

But after carnage there will be music, after death will be hope,

After the horror of the day will come the evening dream,

After hatred's harvest joy will march, shrouded, to Finaghy.

Old Queens Bridge, Belfast (c. 1940s)
Markey Robinson (1917–1999)

BRIGHT AFTER DARK

Pearse Hutchinson

for Sebastian Ryan

In the first country,

what you must do when the cow stops giving milk

is climb, after dark, a certain hill

and play the flute: to kill your scheming neighbour's curse.

If you can find a silver flute to play,

the spell will break all the faster, the surer.

But silver is not essential. But: the job must

be done after dark:

otherwise, it won't work.

In the second country,

when you send a child out of the house at night,

after dark, you must, if you wish it well,

take, from the fire, a burnt-out cinder

and place it on the palm of the child's hand

to guard the child against the dangers of the dark.

The cinder, in this good function, is called aingeal,

meaning angel.

In the third country,

if you take a journey at night, above all

in the blind night of ebony, so good for witches to work in,

you dare not rely on fireflies for light,

for theirs is a brief, inconstant glow. What you must hope

is that someone before you has dropped grains of maize

on the ground to light your way; and you must drop

grains of maize for whoever comes after you:

for only maize can light the way on a dark night.

Inishfallen Islands, Killarney, in Moonlight
Patrick Vincent Duffy (1832–1909)

THE MADWOMAN OF CORK
Patrick Galvin

To-day
Is the feast day of Saint Anne
Pray for me
I am the madwoman of Cork.

Yesterday
In Castle Street
I saw two goblins at my feet
I saw a horse without a head
Carrying the dead
To the graveyard
Near Turner's Cross.

I am the madwoman of Cork
No one talks to me.

When I walk in the rain
The children throw stones at me
Old men persecute me
And women close their doors.
When I die
Believe me
They'll set me on fire.

I am the madwoman of Cork
I have no sense.

Sometimes
With an eagle in my brain
I can see a train
Crashing at the station.
If I told people that
They'd choke me—
Then where would I be?

I am the madwoman of Cork
The people hate me.

The Enraged Woman (1977)
Maurice MacGonigal (1900–1979)

When Canon Murphy died
I wept on his grave
That was twenty-five years ago.
When I saw him just now
In Dunbar Street
He had clay in his teeth
He blest me.

I am the madwoman of Cork
The clergy pity me.

I see death
In the branches of a tree
Birth in the feathers of a bird.
To see a child with one eye
Or a woman buried in ice
Is the worst thing
And cannot be imagined.

I am the madwoman of Cork
My mind fills me.

I should like to be young
To dress up in silk
And have nine children.
I'd like to have red lips
But I'm eighty years old
I have nothing
But a small house with no windows.

I am the madwoman of Cork
Go away from me.

And if I die now
Don't touch me.
I want to sail in a long boat
From here to Roche's Point
And there I will anoint the sea
With oil of alabaster.

I am the madwoman of Cork
And to-day is the feast day of Saint Anne.
Feed me.

THE READING LESSON
Richard Murphy

Fourteen years old, learning the alphabet,
He finds letters harder to catch than hares
Without a greyhound. Can't I give him a dog
To track them down, or put them in a cage?
He's caught in a trap, until I let him go,
Pinioned by 'Don't you want to learn to read?'
'I'll be the same man whatever I do.'

He looks at a page as a mule balks at a gap
From which a goat may hobble out and bleat.
His eyes jink from a sentence like flushed snipe
Escaping shot. A sharp word, and he'll mooch
Back to his piebald mare and bantam cock.
Our purpose is as tricky to retrieve
As mercury from a smashed thermometer.

'I'll not read anymore.' Should I give up?
His hands, long-fingered as a Celtic scribe's,
Will grow callous, gathering sticks or scrap;
Exploring pockets of the horny drunk
Loiterers at the fairs, giving them lice.
A neighbour chuckles. 'You can never tame
The wild duck: when his wings grow, he'll fly off.'

If books resembled roads, he'd quickly read:
But they're small farms to him, fenced by the page,
Ploughed into lines, with letters drilled like oats:
A field of tasks he'll always be outside.
If words were bank-notes, he would filch a wad;
If they were pheasants, they'd be in his pot
For breakfast, or if wrens he'd make them king.

Landscape with Pheasants through a Bank of Flowers
Andrew Nicholl (1804–1886)

HIS FATHER'S HANDS

Thomas Kinsella

I drank firmly
and set the glass down between us firmly.
You were saying.

My father
Was saying.

His finger prodded and prodded,
marring his point. Emphas-
emphasemphasis.

I have watched
his father's hands before him

    cupped, and tightening the black Plug
between knife and thumb,
carving off little curlicues
to rub them in the dark of his palms,

or cutting into new leather at his bench,
levering a groove open with his thumb,
insinuating wet sprigs for the hammer.

He kept the sprigs in mouthfuls
and brought them out in silvery
units between his lips.

I took a pinch out of their hole
and knocked them one by one into the wood,
bright points among hundreds gone black,
other children's – cousins and others, grown up.

    Or his bow hand scarcely moving,
scraping in the dark corner near the fire,
his plump fingers shifting on the strings.

To his deaf, inclined head
he hugged the fiddle's body
whispering with the tune

with breaking heart
whene'er I hear
in privacy, across a blocked void,

the wind that shakes the barley.
The wind …
round her grave …

on my breast in blood she died …
But blood for blood without remorse
I've ta'en …

Beyond that.

★ ★ ★

A Quiet Whiff
Henry Wright Kerr (1857–1936)

Your family, Thomas, met with and helped
many of the Croppies in hiding from the Yeos
or on their way home after the defeat
in south Wexford. They sheltered the Laceys
who were later hanged on the Bridge in Ballinglen
between Tinahely and Anacorra.

From hearsay, as far as I can tell
the Men Folk were either Stone Cutters
or masons or probably both.
                              In the 18
and late 1700s even the farmers
had some other trade to make a living.

They lived in Farnese among a Colony
of North of Ireland or Scotch settlers left there
in some of the dispersals or migrations
which occurred in this Area of Wicklow and Wexford
and Carlow. And some years before that time
the Family came from somewhere around Tullow.

Beyond that.

★　★　★

Littered uplands. Dense grass. Rocks everywhere,
wet underneath, retaining memory of the long cold.

First, a prow of land
chosen, and wedged with tracks;
then boulders chosen
and sloped together, stabilized in menace.

I do not like this place.
I do not think the people who lived here
were ever happy. It feels evil.
Terrible things happened.
I feel afraid here when I am on my own.

★　★　★

Dispersals or migrations.
Through what evolutions or accidents
toward that peace and patience
by the fireside, that blocked gentleness …

That serene pause, with the slashing knife,
in kindly mockery,
as I busy myself with my little nails
at the rude block, his bench.

The Stone Cutter
Martin Driscoll (1945–)

The blood advancing
– gorging vessel after vessel –
and altering in them
one by one.

Behold, that gentleness already
modulated twice, in others:
to earnestness and iteration;
to an offhandedness, repressing various impulses.

★ ★ ★

Extraordinary … The big block – I found it
years afterward in a corner of the yard
in sunlight after rain
and stood it up, wet and black:
it turned under my hands, an axis
of light flashing down its length,
and the wood's soft flesh broke open,
countless little nails
squirming and dropping out of it.

LIKE DOLMENS ROUND MY CHILDHOOD, THE OLD PEOPLE

John Montague

Like dolmens round my childhood, the old people.

Jamie MacCrystal sang to himself,

A broken song without tune, without words;

He tipped me a penny every pension day,

Fed kindly crusts to winter birds.

When he died, his cottage was robbed,

Mattress and money box torn and searched.

Only the corpse they didn't disturb.

Maggie Owens was surrounded by animals,

A mongrel bitch and shivering pups,

Even in her bedroom a she-goat cried.

She was a well of gossip defiled,

Fanged chronicler of a whole countryside:

Reputed a witch, all I could find

Was her lonely need to deride.

The Quaint Couple
Charles Vincent Lamb (1893–1964)

The Nialls lived along a mountain lane
Where heather bells bloomed, clumps of foxglove.
All were blind, with Blind Pension and Wireless,
Dead eyes serpent-flicked as one entered
To shelter from a downpour of mountain rain.
Crickets chirped under the rocking hearthstone
Until the muddy sun shone out again.

Mary Moore lived in a crumbling gatehouse,
Famous as Pisa for its leaning gable.
Bag-apron and boots, she tramped the fields
Driving lean cattle from a miry stable.
A by-word for fierceness, she fell asleep
Over love stories, *Red Star* and *Red Circle*,
Dreamed of gypsy love rites, by firelight sealed.

Wild Billy Eagleson married a Catholic servant girl
When all his Loyal family passed on:
We danced round him shouting 'To Hell with King Billy,'
And dodged from the arc of his flailing blackthorn.
Forsaken by both creeds, he showed little concern
Until the Orange drums banged past in the summer
And bowler and sash aggressively shone.

Old People Watching a Dance
Paul Henry (1876–1958)

Curate and doctor trudged to attend them,

Through knee-deep snow, through summer heat,

From main road to lane to broken path,

Gulping the mountain air with painful breath.

Sometimes they were found by neighbours,

Silent keepers of a smokeless hearth,

Suddenly cast in the mould of death.

Ancient Ireland, indeed! I was reared by her bedside,

The rune and the chant, evil eye and averted head,

Fomorian fierceness of family and local feud.

Gaunt figures of fear and of friendliness,

For years they trespassed on my dreams,

Until once, in a standing circle of stones,

I felt their shadows pass

Into that dark permanence of ancient forms.

Stone Circle
Carmel Mooney (1962–)

CLAUDY

James Simmons

for Harry Barton, a song

The Sperrins surround it, the Faughan flows by,
at each end of Main Street the hills and the sky,
the small town of Claudy at ease in the sun
last July in the morning, a new day begun.

How peaceful and pretty if the moment could stop,
McIlhenny is straightening things in his shop,
and his wife is outside serving petrol, and then
a girl takes a cloth to a big window pane.

And McCloskey is taking the weight off his feet,
and McClelland and Miller are sweeping the street,
and, delivering milk at the Beaufort Hotel,
young Temple's enjoying his first job quite well.

And Mrs McLaughlin is scrubbing her floor,
and Artie Hone's crossing the street to a door,
and Mrs Brown, looking around for her cat,
goes off up an entry – what's strange about that?

Not much – but before she comes back to the road
that strange car parked outside her house will explode,
and all of the people I've mentioned outside
will be waiting to die or already have died.

Adam and Eve (c.1969)
Patrick Collins (1911–1994)

An explosion too loud for your eardrums to bear,
and young children squealing like pigs in the square,
and all faces chalk-white and streaked with bright red,
and the glass and the dust and the terrible dead.

For an old lady's legs are blown off, and the head
of a man's hanging open, and still he's not dead.
He is screaming for mercy, and his son stands and stares
and stares, and then suddenly, quick, disappears.

And Christ, little Katherine Aiken is dead,
and Mrs McLaughlin is pierced through the head.
Meanwhile to Dungiven the killers have gone,
and they're finding it hard to get through on the phone.

Old Woman and Washing (c. 1959–60)
Gerard Dillon (1916–1971)

DIGGING

Seamus Heaney

Between my finger and my thumb
The squat pen rests; snug as a gun.

Under my window, a clean rasping sound
When the spade sinks into gravelly ground:
My father, digging. I look down

Till his straining rump among the flowerbeds
Bends low, comes up twenty years away
Stooping in rhythm through potato drills
Where he was digging.

The coarse boot nestled on the lug, the shaft
Against the inside knee was levered firmly.
He rooted out tall tops, buried the bright edge deep
To scatter new potatoes that we picked,
Loving their cool hardness in our hands.

By God, the old man could handle a spade,
Just like his old man.

My grandfather cut more turf in a day
Than any other man on Toner's bog.
Once I carried him milk in a bottle
Corked sloppily with paper. He straightened up
To drink it, then fell to right away
Nicking and slicing neatly, heaving sods
Over his shoulder, going down and down
For the good turf. Digging.

The cold smell of potato mould, the squelch and slap
Of soggy peat, the curt cuts of an edge
Through living roots awaken in my head.
But I've no spade to follow men like them.

Between my finger and my thumb
The squat pen rests.
I'll dig with it.

The Potato Diggers
Paul Henry (1876–1958)

MID-TERM BREAK

Seamus Heaney

I sat all morning in the college sick bay
Counting bells knelling classes to a close.
At two o'clock our neighbours drove me home.

In the porch I met my father crying –
He had always taken funerals in his stride –
And Big Jim Evans saying it was a hard blow.

The baby cooed and laughed and rocked the pram
When I came in, and I was embarrassed
By old men standing up to shake my hand

And tell me they were 'sorry for my trouble.'
Whispers informed strangers I was the eldest,
Away at school, as my mother held my hand

In hers and coughed out angry tearless sighs.
At ten o'clock the ambulance arrived
With the corpse, stanched and bandaged by the nurses.

Next morning I went up into the room. Snowdrops
And candles soothed the bedside; I saw him
For the first time in six weeks. Paler now,

Wearing a poppy bruise on his left temple,
He lay in the four-foot box as in his cot.
No gaudy scars, the bumper knocked him clear.

A four-foot box, a foot for every year.

Head of a Boy (c.1940)
Evie Hone (1894–1955)

DERRY DERRY DOWN

Seamus Heaney

I
The lush
Sunset blush
On a big ripe

Gooseberry:
I scratched my hand
Reaching in

To gather it
Off the bush,
Unforbidden,

In Annie Devlin's
Overgrown
Back garden.

II
In the storybook
Back kitchen
Of The Lodge

The full of a white
Enamel bucket
Of little pears:

Still life
On the red tiles
Of that floor.

Sleeping beauty
I came on
By the scullion's door.

Grandpa's Garden
Rose Maynard Barton (1856–1929)

CEASEFIRE

Michael Longley

I

Put in mind of his own father and moved to tears
Achilles took him by the hand and pushed the old king
Gently away, but Priam curled up at his feet and
Wept with him until their sadness filled the building.

II

Taking Hector's corpse into his own hands Achilles
Made sure it was washed and, for the old king's sake,
Laid out in uniform, ready for Priam to carry
Wrapped like a present home to Troy at daybreak.

III

When they had eaten together, it pleased them both
To stare at each other's beauty as lovers might,
Achilles built like a god, Priam good-looking still
And full of conversation, who earlier had sighed:

IV

'I get down on my knees and do what must be done
And kiss Achilles' hand, the killer of my son.'

The Education of Achilles (c.1772)
James Barry (1741–1806)

DERRY MORNING

Derek Mahon

The mist clears and the cavities
Glow black in the rubbled city's
Broken mouth. An early crone,
Muse of a fitful revolution
Wasted by the fray, she sees
Her *aisling* falter in the breeze,
Her oak-grove vision hesitate
By empty wharf and city gate.

Here it began, and here at last
It fades into the finite past
Or seems to: clattering shadows whop
Mechanically over pub and shop.
A strangely pastoral silence rules
The shining roofs and murmuring schools;
For this is how the centuries work —
Two steps forward, one step back.

Hard to believe this tranquil place,
Its desolation almost peace,
Was recently a boom-town wild
With expectation, each unscheduled
Incident a measurable
Tremor on the Richter Scale
Of world events, each vibrant scene
Translated to the drizzling screen.

What of the change envisioned here,
The quantum leap from fire to fear?
Smoke from a thousand chimneys strains
One way beneath the returning rains
That shroud the bomb-sites, while the fog
Of time receives the ideologue.
A Russian freighter bound for home
Mourns to the city in its gloom.

Light of the World Martyrs of the Vision of St John
Colin Middleton (1910–1983)

A Disused Shed in Co. Wexford

Derek Mahon

Let them not forget us, the weak souls among the asphodels.   (Seferis, *Mythistorema*)

for J. G. Farrell

Even now there are places where a thought might grow –
Peruvian mines, worked out and abandoned
To a slow clock of condensation,
An echo trapped for ever, and a flutter
Of wildflowers in the lift-shaft,
Indian compounds where the wind dances
And a door bangs with diminished confidence,
Lime crevices behind rippling rainbarrels,
Dog corners for bone burials;
And in a disused shed in Co. Wexford,

Deep in the grounds of a burnt-out hotel,
Among the bathtubs and the washbasins
A thousand mushrooms crowd to a keyhole.
This is the one star in their firmament
Or frames a star within a star.
What should they do there but desire?
So many days beyond the rhododendrons
With the world waltzing in its bowl of cloud,
They have learnt patience and silence
Listening to the rooks querulous in the high wood.

They have been waiting for us in a foetor
Of vegetable sweat since civil war days,
Since the gravel-crunching, interminable departure
Of the expropriated mycologist.
He never came back, and light since then
Is a keyhole rusting gently after rain.
Spiders have spun, flies dusted to mildew
And once a day, perhaps, they have heard something –
A trickle of masonry, a shout from the blue
Or a lorry changing gear at the end of the lane.

There have been deaths, the pale flesh flaking
Into the earth that nourished it;
And nightmares, born of these and the grim
Dominion of stale air and rank moisture.
Those nearest the door grow strong –
'Elbow room! Elbow room!'
The rest, dim in a twilight of crumbling
Utensils and broken pitchers, groaning
For their deliverance, have been so long
Expectant that there is left only the posture.

Under the Pier (c. 1959)
Patrick Scott (1921–)

A half century, without visitors, in the dark –

Poor preparation for the cracking lock

And creak of hinges. Magi, moonmen,

Powdery prisoners of the old regime,

Web-throated, stalked like triffids, racked by drought

And insomnia, only the ghost of a scream

At the flash-bulb firing squad we wake them with

Shows there is life yet in their feverish forms.

Grown beyond nature now, soft food for worms,

They lift frail heads in gravity and good faith.

They are begging us, you see, in their wordless way,

To do something, to speak on their behalf

Or at least not to close the door again.

Lost people of Treblinka and Pompeii!

'Save us, save us,' they seem to say,

'Let the god not abandon us

Who have come so far in darkness and in pain.

We too had our lives to live.

You with your light meter and relaxed itinerary,

Let not our naive labours have been in vain!'

ANTARCTICA

Derek Mahon

'I am just going outside and may be some time.'
The others nod, pretending not to know.
At the heart of the ridiculous, the sublime.

He leaves them reading and begins to climb,
Goading his ghost into the howling snow;
He is just going outside and may be some time.

The tent recedes beneath its crust of rime
And frostbite is replaced by vertigo:
At the heart of the ridiculous, the sublime.

Need we consider it some sort of crime,
This numb self-sacrifice of the weakest? No,
He is just going outside and may be some time –

In fact, for ever. Solitary enzyme,
Though the night yield no glimmer there will glow,
At the heart of the ridiculous, the sublime.

He takes leave of the earthly pantomime
Quietly, knowing it is time to go:
'I am just going outside and may be some time.'
At the heart of the ridiculous, the sublime.

Bergy Bits, Antarctica
Vicki Crowley (1940–)

DEATH OF AN IRISHWOMAN
Michael Hartnett

Ignorant, in the sense
she ate monotonous food
and thought the world was flat,
and pagan, in the sense
she knew the things that moved
all night were neither dogs nor cats
but púcas and darkfaced men
she nevertheless had fierce pride.
But sentenced in the end
to eat thin diminishing porridge
in a stone-cold kitchen
she clenched her brittle hands
around a world
she could not understand.
I loved her from the day she died.
She was a summer dance at the crossroads.
She was a cardgame where a nose was broken.
She was a song that nobody sings.
She was a house ransacked by soldiers.
She was a language seldom spoken.
She was a child's purse, full of useless things.

A Prayer for the Departed
Paul Henry (1876–1958)

A Farewell to English

Michael Hartnett

for Brendan Kennelly

1

Her eyes were coins of porter and her West
Limerick voice talked velvet in the house:
her hair was black as the glossy fireplace
wearing with grace her Sunday-night-dance best.
She cut the froth from glasses with a knife
and hammered golden whiskies on the bar
and her mountainy body tripped the gentle
mechanism of verse: the minute interlock
of word and word began, the rhythm formed.
I sunk my hands into tradition
sifting the centuries for words. This quiet
excitement was not new: emotion challenged me
to make it sayable. The clichés came
at first, like matchsticks snapping from the world
of work: mánla, séimh, dubhfholtach, álainn, caoin:
they came like grey slabs of slate breaking from
an ancient quarry, mánia, séimh, dubhfholtach,
álainn, caoin, slowly vaulting down the dark
unused escarpments, mánla, séimh, dubhfholtach,
álainn, caoin, crashing on the cogs, splinters
like axeheads damaged the wheels, clogging
the intricate machine, mánla, séimh,

dubhfholtach, álainn, caoin. Then Pegasus
pulled up, the girth broke and I was flung back
on the gravel of Anglo-Saxon.
What was I doing with these foreign words?
I, the polisher of the complex clause,
wizard of grasses and warlock of birds
midnight-oiled in the metric laws?

Forest (c. *1977*)
Barrie Cooke (1931–)

2

Half afraid to break a promise
made to Dinny Halpin Friday night
I sat down from my walk to Camas
Sunday evening, Doody's Cross,
and took off my burning boots
on a gentle bench of grass.
The cows had crushed the evening
green with mint:
springwater from the roots
of a hawkfaced firtree on my right
swamped pismires bringing home
their sweet supplies
and strawberries looked out
with ferrets' eyes.
These old men walked on the summer road
súgán belts and long black coats
with big ashplants and half-sacks
of rags and bacon on their backs.
They stopped before me with a knowing look
hungry, snotnosed, half-drunk.
I said 'grand evening'

and they looked at me awhile
then took their roads
to Croom, Meentogues and Cahirmoyle.
They look back once,
black moons of misery
sickling their eye-sockets,
a thousand years of history
in their pockets.

3

Chef Yeats, that master of the use of herbs
could raise mere stew to a glorious height,
pinch of saga, soupçon of philosophy
carefully stirred in to get the flavour right,
and cook a poem around the basic verbs.
Our commis-chefs attend and learn the trade,
bemoan the scraps of Gaelic that they know:
add to a simple Anglo-Saxon stock
Cuchulainn's marrow-bones to marinate,
a dash of Ó Rathaille simmered slow,
a glass of University hic-haec-hoc:
sniff and stand back and proudly offer you
the celebrated Anglo-Irish stew.

4

We woke one morning
in a Dublin digs
and found we were descended
from two pigs.
The brimming Irish sow
who would allow
any syphilitic boar
to make her hind-end sore
was Mammy.
Daddy was an English boar
who wanted nothing
but a sweaty rut
and ownership of any offspring.
We knew we had been robbed
but were not sure that we lost
the right to have a language
or the right to be the boss.

So we queued up at the Castle
in nineteen-twenty-two
to make our Gaelic
or our Irish dream come true.

We could have had from that start
made certain of our fate
but we chose to learn the noble art
of writing forms in triplicate.
With big wide eyes
and childish smiles
quivering on our lips
we enterered the Irish paradise
of files and paper-clips.

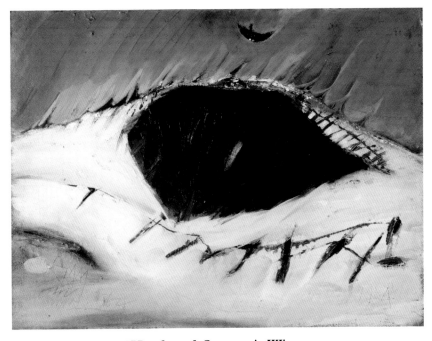

Hawk and Quarry in Winter
Tony O'Malley (1913–2003)

5

I say farewell to English verse,
to those I found in English nets:
my Lorca holding out his arms
to love the beauty of his bullets,
Pasternak who outlived Stalin
and died because of lesser beasts:
to all the poets I have loved
from Wyatt to Robert Browning:
to Father Hopkins in his crowded grave
and to our bugbear Mr Yeats
who forced us into exile
on islands of bad verse.

Among my living friends
there is no poet I do not love,
although some write
with bitterness in their hearts:
they are one art, our many arts.
Poets with progress
make no peace or pact:
the act of poetry
is a rebel act.

6

Gaelic is the conscience of our leaders,
the memory of a mother-rape they will
not face, the heap of bloody rags they see
and scream at in their boardrooms of mock oak.
They push us towards the world of total work,
our politicians with their seedy minds
and dubious labels, Communist or
Capitalist, none wanting freedom —
only power. All that reminds us
we are human and therefore not a herd
must be concealed or killed or slowly left
to die, or microfilmed to waste no space.
For Gaelic is our final sign that
we are human, therefore not a herd.

Hog Heaven
Martin Driscoll (1945–)

I saw our governments the other night —
I think the scene was Leopardstown —
horribly deformed dwarfs rode the racetrack
each mounted on a horribly deformed dwarf:
greenfaced, screaming, yellow-toothed, prodding
each other with electric prods, thrashing
each others' skinny arses, dribbling snot
and smeared with their own dung, they galloped
towards the prize, a glass and concrete anus.

I think the result was a dead heat.

Tinkers Gathering Firewood (c.1950)
Nano Reid (1905–1981)

7

This road is not new.
I am not a maker of new things.
I cannot hew
out of the vacuumcleaner minds
the sense of serving dead kings.

I am nothing new
I am not a lonely mouth
trying to chew
a niche for culture
in the clergy-cluttered south.

But I will not see
great men go down
who walked in rags
from town to town
finding English a necessary sin
the perfect language to sell pigs in.

I have made my choice
and leave with little weeping:
I have come with meagre voice
to court the language of my people.

THE SECOND VOYAGE
Eiléan Ní Chuilleanáin

Odysseus rested on his oar and saw
The ruffled foreheads of the waves
Crocodiling and mincing past: he rammed
The oar between their jaws and looked down
In the simmering sea where scribbles of weeds defined
Uncertain depth, and the slim fishes progressed
In fatal formation, and thought

                    If there was a single
Streak of decency in these waves now, they'd be ridged
Pocked and dented with the battering they've had,
And we could name them as Adam named the beasts,
Saluting a new one with dismay, or a notorious one
With admiration; they'd notice us passing
And rejoice at our shipwreck, but these
Have less character than sheep and need more patience.

I know what I'll do he said;
I'll park my ship in the crook of a long pier
(And I'll take you with me he said to the oar)
I'll face the rising ground and walk away
From tidal waters, up river beds
Where herons parcel out the miles of stream,

The Man from the West: Sean Keating
William Orpen (1878–1931)

Over gaps in the hills, through warm

Silent valleys, and when I meet a farmer

Bold enough to look me in the eye

With 'where are you off to with that long

Winnowing fan over your shoulder?'

There I will stand still

And I'll plant you for a gatepost or a hitching-post

And leave you as a tidemark. I can go back

And organise my house then.

But the profound

Unfenced valleys of the ocean still held him;

He had only the oar to make them keep their distance;

The sea was still frying under the ship's side.

He considered the water-lilies, and thought about fountains

Spraying as wide as willows in empty squares,

The sugarstick of water clattering into the kettle,

The flat lakes bisecting the rushes. He remembered spiders and frogs

Housekeeping at the roadside in brown trickles floored with mud,

Horsetroughs, the black canal, pale swans at dark:

His face grew damp with tears that tasted

Like his own sweat or the insults of the sea.

FIRE AND SNOW AND CARNEVALE
Macdara Woods

In winter fire is beautiful
beautiful like music
it lights the cave —
outside the people going home
drive slowly up the road — the strains
of phone-in Verdi on the radio
three hours back a fall of snow
sprinkled the furthest hill
where clouds have hung all winter

The day gets dark uneasy
dark and darker still
and you little son come home
riding the tail of the wind
in triumph — tall and almost ten
with confetti in your hair
home successful from the carnevale
with your two black swords
and your gold-handled knife

I feel the chill and hear
the absent sound of snow
when you come in —
while fantastic scorpions spit
in the fiery centre of the grate
plague pictures cauterised —
In winter fire is beautiful
and generous as music — may you
always come this safely home
in fire and snow and carnevale

Snow Covered Landscape (1952)
Daniel O'Neill (1920–1974)

NIGHT FEED

Eavan Boland

This is dawn.

Believe me

This is your season, little daughter.

The moment daisies open,

The hour mercurial rainwater

Makes a mirror for sparrows.

It's time we drowned our sorrows.

I tiptoe in.

I lift you up

Wriggling

In your rosy, zipped sleeper.

Yes, this is the hour

For the early bird and me

When finder is keeper.

I crook the bottle.

How you suckle!

This is the best I can be,

Housewife

To this nursery

Where you hold on,

Dear life.

A silt of milk.

The last suck.

And now your eyes are open,

Birth-coloured and offended.

Earth wakes.

You go back to sleep.

The feed is ended.

Worms turn.

Stars go in.

Even the moon is losing face.

Poplars stilt for dawn

And we begin

The long fall from grace.

I tuck you in.

The Mother
John Lavery (1856–1941)

IRISH HIERARCHY BANS COLOUR PHOTOGRAPHY

Paul Durcan

After a Spring meeting in their nineteenth-century fastness at Maynooth

The Irish Hierarchy has issued a total ban on the practice of colour photography:

A spokesman added that while in accordance with tradition

No logical explanation would be provided

There were a number of illogical explanations which he would discuss;

He stated that it was not true that the ban was the result

Of the Hierarchy's tacit endorsement of racial discrimination;

(And, here, the spokesman, Fr Marksman, smiled to himself

But when asked to elaborate on his smile, he would not elaborate

Except to growl some categorical expletives which included the word 'liberal')

He stated that if the Press corps would countenance an unhappy pun

He would say that negative thinking lay at the root of the ban;

Colour pictures produced in the minds of people,

Especially in the minds (if any) of young people,

A serious distortion of reality;

Colour pictures showed reality to be rich and various

Whereas reality in point of fact was the opposite;

The innate black and white nature of reality would have to be safeguarded

At all costs and, talking of costs, said Fr Marksman,

It ought to be borne in mind, as indeed the Hierarchy had borne in its collective mind,

That colour photography was far costlier than black and white photography

And, as a consequence, more immoral;

The Hierarchy, stated Fr Marksman, was once again smiting two birds with one boulder;

And the joint-hegemony of Morality and Economics was being upheld.

The total ban came as a total surprise to the accumulated Press corps

And Irish Roman Catholic pressmen and presswomen present

Had to be helped away as they wept copiously in their cups:

'No more oranges and lemons in Maynooth' sobbed one cameraboy.

The general public, however, is expected to pay no heed to the ban;

Only politicians and time-servers are likely to pay the required lip-service;

But the operative noun is lip: there will be no hand or foot service.

And next year Ireland is expected to become

The EEC's largest money-spender in colour photography:

This is Claudia Conway RTE News (Colour) Maynooth.

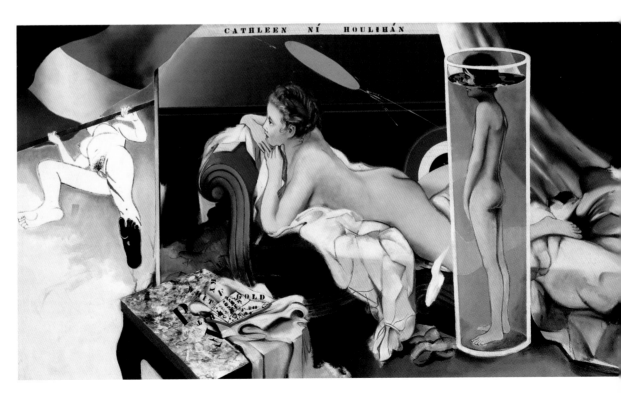

Cathleen Ni Houlihan
(Madonna Irlanda)
Michael Farrell (1940–2000)

SILENCE

Biddy Jenkinson

How I welcome you, little salmon
who leapt the womb, impatient to commence life.
I undertake to be a river to you
as you follow your course from the haven of
    my belly to far distant seas.

Let yourself go, and drink up your fill.
Suck sleep from me. By the terms of the breast-contract
I'll suck back from your puckered lips
love, with which I'll suckle another time, and for that
    I'm grateful.

How I welcome you, salmon of sleep
who made a tranquil pool in my life-stream.
In the rhythm of your heartbeat
I hear the music of the Heavens,
    and it guides my way.

Translated by Pádraigín Riggs

Mother
Luke Lawnicki (1966–)

THE APHRODISIAC
Medbh McGuckian

She gave it out as if it were

A marriage or a birth, some other

Interesting family event, that she

Had finished sleeping with him, that

Her lover was her friend. It was his heart

She wanted, the bright key to his study,

Not the menacings of love. So he is

Banished to his estates, to live

Like a man in a glasshouse; she has taken to

A little cap of fine white lace

In the mornings, feeds her baby

In a garden you could visit blindfold

For its scent alone:

               But though a ray of grace

Has fallen, all her books seem as frumpish

As the last year's gambling game, when she

Would dress in pink taffeta, and drive

A blue phaeton, or in blue, and drive

A pink one, with her black hair supported

By a diamond comb, floating about

Without panniers. How his most

Caressing look, his husky whisper suffocates her,

This almost perfect power of knowing

More than a kept woman. The between-maid

Tells me this is not the only secret staircase.

Rumour has it she's taken to rouge again.

St Finbarre (c. *1978*)
Alicia Boyle (1908–1997)

CUBA

Paul Muldoon

My eldest sister arrived home that morning
In her white muslin evening dress.
'Who the hell do you think you are,
Running out to dances in next to nothing?
As though we hadn't enough bother
With the world at war, if not at an end.'
My father was pounding the breakfast-table.

'Those Yankees were touch and go as it was –
If you'd heard Patton in Armagh –
But this Kennedy's nearly an Irishman
So he's not much better than ourselves.
And him with only to say the word.
If you've got anything on your mind
Maybe you should make your peace with God.'

I could hear May from beyond the curtain.
'Bless me, Father, for I have sinned.
I told a lie once, I was disobedient once.
And, Father, a boy touched me once.'
'Tell me, child. Was this touch immodest?
Did he touch your breast, for example?'
'He brushed against me, Father. Very gently.'

*Night Odyssey (*c. *1960)*
John O'Leary (1929–1999)

BLODEWEDD

Nuala Ní Dhomhnaill

At the least touch of your fingertips
I break into blossom,
my whole chemical composition
transformed.
I sprawl like a grassy meadow
fragrant in the sun;
at the brush of your palm, all my herbs
and spices spill open

frond by frond, lured to unfold
and exhale in the heat;
wild strawberries rife, and pimpernels
flagrant and scarlet, blushing
down their stems.
To mow that rushy bottom;
no problem.

All winter I waited silently
for your appeal.
I withered within, dead to all,
curled away, and deaf as clay,
all my life forces ebbing slowly
till now I come to, at your touch,
revived as from a deathly swoon.

Your sun lightens my sky
and a wind lifts, like God's angel,
to move the waters,
every inch of me quivers
before your presence,
goose-pimples I get as you glide
over me, and every hair
stands on end.

Hours later I linger
in the ladies toilet,
a sweet scent wafting
from all my pores,
proof positive, if a sign
were needed, that at the least
touch of your fingertips
I break into blossom.

Translated by John Montague

Summer Fields, Donegal
Robert Bottom (1944–)

THE PHENOMENOLOGY OF STONES

Thomas McCarthy

for Catherine

These summer days I carry images of stone,
Small pebbles from a photographer's shelf
Made smooth by a million years of sea and salt.
Sunlight shines roundly into their small room,
Twisting black grains into crystals and gems:
Lights call like young birds from their surfaces,
Sparrows of light flying from graves, from places
Where the dead had grown; the sorrow-gardens.

But the silence of stone quietens the mind
And calms the eye. Like their girl-collector –
In her deep solitude the stones are moved.
She is their dream-collector, pouring her kind-
ness into their sleeping form. They gather
Fables about themselves to entertain such love.

Floating Stones
Patrick Walshe (1952–)

Poets' Biographies

William Allingham (1824–1889), born in Ballyshannon, Co. Donegal, was a poet and editor. Amongst his major works is 'Laurence Bloomfield in Ireland', written in 1864, a lengthy poem about land agitation. His other works include *Fifty Modern Poems* (1865), *Songs, Poems, and Ballads* (1877), *Evil May Day* (1883), *Blackberries* (1884), and *Irish Songs and Poems* (1887).

Brendan Behan (1923–1964) was born in Dublin. A poet, short story writer, novelist, and playwright, he was also an Irish republican and a volunteer in the Irish Republican Army. His mother, Kathleen, was a personal friend of the Irish republican Michael Collins to whom Behan wrote a lament, 'The Laughing Boy', at the age of thirteen. In 1937 Behan became a member of Fianna Éireann, the youth organisation of the IRA. He published his first poems and prose in the organisation's magazine, *Fianna: the Voice of Young Ireland*. At sixteen, Behan joined the IRA. His prison experiences included fourteen years in Mountjoy Prison, which led to his writing 'Confessions of an Irish Rebel'. Behan was a heavy drinker and described himself, on one occasion, as 'a drinker with a writing problem'. He found fame difficult and as fame grew so did his alcohol consumption, which ultimately led to his death at the age of 41.

Eavan Boland (1944–) was born in Dublin and educated at Trinity College. A poet and academic, she is a pioneering feminist writer. Amongst her works are 'The War Horse' (1975), 'In Her Own Image' (1980), 'Night

Feed' (1982) and *Outside History, Selected Poems 1980–1990* (1990).

Joseph Campbell (1879–1944), poet, lyricist, journalist and nationalist activist, was born in Belfast and educated at St Malachy's College, Belfast. He was a founder of the Ulster Literary Theatre in 1904 and edited *Uladh*, the theatre's journal. He is remembered for the words he supplied to traditional airs such as 'My Lagan Love' and 'Gartan Mother's Lullaby'; some of his verse was also set to music.

Ethna Carbery (1866–1902) was the pen-name of the Irish poet Anna MacManus, née Johnston, born in Ballymena, Co. Antrim. A poet and writer, she was a nationalist political activist and produced poetry and novels. Her publications include *The Four Winds of Eirinn* (1902), a book of poetry, *The Passionate Hearts* (1903), a collection of short stories, and *In the Celtic Past* (1904).

Austin Clarke (1896–1974) was born in Dublin and educated at University College Dublin. A leading poet, he also wrote plays, novels and memoirs. He co-founded the Lyric Theatre and pioneered the idea of verse plays for radio as a founder of the Dublin Verse-Speaking Society. Clarke set up the Bridge Press to publish his own work, and in 1974 published his *Collected Poems*, followed by *Selected Poems* in 1976.

Padraic Colum (1881–1972), born in Co. Longford, was a poet, playwright, dramatist, biographer, novelist and folklorist. He had

a long career as a writer in Ireland and the United States, and was a member of the first board of the Abbey Theatre. His collection of Irish folk songs included the famous 'She Moved Through the Fair', for which he wrote most of the words.

Maurice James Craig (1919–2011) was born in Belfast and educated at Trinity College and Cambridge. A poet and architectural historian, his books have become definitive of their topics: *Dublin 1660–1860* (1952) and *Classic Irish Houses of the Middle Size* (1976).

Leslie Daiken (1912–1964) was born in Dublin and educated at Trinity College. He served in the Irish army during the Second World War, and was special correspondent for Reuters. He edited anthologies of socialist poetry and published volumes of his own work: *The Signature of all Things* (1944) and *The Lullaby Book* (1957).

Thomas Davis (1814–1845) was born in Mallow, Co. Cork and educated at Trinity College, Dublin. He graduated in law and was called to the Irish Bar in 1838, but he never practised. In 1842 he co-founded the *Nation*, a weekly newspaper, and in the three years that he worked on the paper he wrote over eighty songs and ballads. From 1842 to 1845 he was leader of the Young Ireland movement. Among his works are the Irish rebel song 'A Nation Once Again', and the 'Lament for Owen Roe O'Neill'.

Mary Devenport O'Neill (1879–1967) was born in Galway and studied at the

National College of Art, Dublin. She wrote two verse plays produced by the Lyric Theatre Company – *Bluebeard* (1933) and *Cain* (1945). She published regularly in *The Dublin Magazine* and held a literary salon at her home in Rathgar.

William Drennan (1754–1820) was born in Belfast and educated as a doctor in Glasgow and Edinburgh. A physician, poet and pamphleteer, he was a founder of the United Irishmen, devoted to political reform rather than radical action. He founded and edited the literary periodical the *Belfast Magazine*. He is best remembered for his poem 'The Wake of William Orr', written in memory of the executed United Irishman.

Eibhlín Dhubh Ní Chonaill (*c*.1743– *c*.1800) was a member of 'The Liberator' Daniel O'Connell's landed family. Scholars dispute whether the 'Lament for Art O'Leary' was actually written by his widow, or is an outstanding example of a traditional literary form, composed collectively.

Lord Dunsany (Edward Plunkett, 18th Baron of Dunsany) (1878–1957) was born in London but lived much of his life at Dunsany Castle near Tara. A prolific writer of poetry, mythological tales and fantasy, he served in the Boer War and the First World War. He was involved with the Irish Literary Revival and was a major donor to the Abbey Theatre.

Paul Durcan (1944–) was born in Dublin and educated at University College Cork. A poet and social satirist, his distinct poetic voice has established him as a significant commentator on public and private life. Two singular collections, *Crazy About Women* (1991), and *Give me Your Hand* (1994), are based on the art collections of the National Galleries of Dublin and London.

Gerald Fitzgerald, 3rd Earl of Desmond (*d*.1398) was a poet and mathematician. As justiciar of Ireland between 1367 and 1369, he was upholder of the King's authority in the province of Munster. He died (or possibly disappeared) in 1398.

Percy French (1854–1920) was born in Co. Roscommon but spent much of his childhood in France. He studied engineering at Trinity College, where he spent a lot of time song writing and painting watercolours, he considered the latter to be his true vocation. His love of music and the theatre led to his performances as a music hall minstrel. His witty stories and humorous popular songs satirising country life were popular with audiences of the time.

Patrick Galvin (1927–2011) was born in Cork. A poet and playwright, he wrote a number of volumes of acclaimed autobiography including *Song of a Poor Boy* (1989) and *Song for a Raggy Boy* (1991). He is noted in particular for his poem 'The Mad Woman of Cork'. His work was strongly influenced by urban folklore and the ballad tradition. Between 1974 and 1978 he was playwright in residence at the Lyric Theatre, Belfast.

Oliver Goldsmith (*c*.1730–1774) was probably born in Pallas, near Ballymahon in Co. Longford. Educated at Trinity College, he was equally successful as a novelist, poet and playwright. His major works are *The Vicar of Wakefield* (1766), 'The Deserted Village' (1770; written in memory of his brother) and *She Stoops to Conquer* (1773).

Robert Greacen (1920–2008) was born in Derry and educated at Methodist College Belfast and Trinity College Dublin. A poet and anthologist, he spent much of his life in London. He published many poetry collections including *The Bird* (1941), *Northern Harvest* (1944), *The Undying Day* (1948), *A Garland for Captain Fox* (1975), *Young Mr Gibbon* (1979), *A Bright Mask*, (1985), *Carnival at The River* (1990), *Collected Poems* (1995), *Lunch at the Ivy* (Lagan Press, 2002), and *Selected and New Poems* (2006).

Michael Hartnett (1941–1999) was born in Croom, Co. Limerick, and educated at University College Dublin. He was a poet and translator from Spanish and Irish. His books included *Anatomy of a Cliché* (1964), *Gypsy Ballads* (1974) and *Selected and New Poems* (1994). A memorial festival, Éigse Michael Hartnett, is held annually in Newcastle West, Co. Limerick.

Seamus Heaney (1939–) was born in Mossbawn, Co. Derry and educated at Queens University, Belfast, where he taught. He subsequently became Professor of Rhetoric at Harvard and Professor of Poetry at Oxford, and was the 1995 recipient of the Noble Prize for Literature. His works include

Death of a Naturalist (1966), *The Haw Lantern* (1987) and *Human Chain* (2010).

John Hewitt (1907–1987) was born in Belfast and educated at Queen's University. A poet, polemicist and art curator, he held posts at the Ulster Museum and the Herbert Art Gallery, Coventry. His poetry promoted regionalism as a reaction to the issues of a divided island. His collections include *The Day of the Corncrake* (1969) and *Out of My Time: Poems 1969 to 1974* (1974).

F.R. Higgins (1896–1941) was born in Foxford, Co. Mayo. He worked as a trades union activist, poet and literary editor, becoming managing director of the Abbey Theatre in 1938. He published four volumes of poetry: *Island Blood* (1925), *The Dark Breed* (1927), *Arable Holdings* (1933) and *The Gap of Brightness* (1940).

Pearse Hutchinson (1927–) was born in Glasgow and moved to Dublin as a child. He was educated at University College Dublin. A poet, editor and translator, he has published collections from the Catalan, medieval Gallico-Portuguese and Irish. His works include *Tongue Without Hands* (1963), *Watching the Morning Grow* (1972), *Selected Poems* (1980), *Collected Poems* (2002) and *At Least for a While* (2008).

John Kells Ingram (1823–1907) was born in Templecarne, Co. Donegal, and educated at Trinity College. At the age of sixteen he published sonnets in the *Dublin University Magazine*. An economist, scholar and balladeer, he is remembered for his political

ballad 'The Memory of the Dead', in honour of the Irish Rebellion of 1798.

Biddy Jenkinson (1949–) is an Irish-language poet and playwright. She publishes under a pseudonym and prefers not to have her poems appear in English translations within Ireland. Her poems include 'Uiscí Beatha' (1988) and 'Rogha Dánta' (2000).

Patrick Kavanagh (1904–1967) was born in Inniskeen, Co. Monaghan, to a farming family on a nine-acre holding. He self-educated himself with extensive reading. He began writing verse at a young age, and became a literary journalist, poet and novelist. His major works are *The Green Fool* (1938), 'The Great Hunger' (1942), *Tarry Flynn* (1948) and *Come Dance with Kitty Stobling* (1960).

Thomas Kinsella (1928–) was born in Inchicore, Co. Dublin, and educated at University College Dublin. A poet, anthologist and translator, he spent many years as an academic in the United States. His collections include *Nightwalker and Other Poems* (1968), *Notes from the Land of the Dead* (1972), *Fifteen Dead* (1976) and *Thomas Kinsella: Collected Poems* (1956–2001).

Hon. Emily Lawless (1845–1913) was born at Lyons Castle, Co. Kildare. A novelist and poet of Irish topics, although not involved in the Celtic Revival movement, her novels *Hurrish* (1886) and *Grania* (1892) were influential on British opinion. She wrote nineteen books of fiction, biography, history,

nature studies and poetry, but is most famous nowadays for her 'Wild Geese' poems.

Francis Ledwidge (1887–1917) was born in Slane, Co. Meath. An Irish war poet, sometimes known as the 'poet of the blackbirds', his poetry is concerned with the nature and mythology of his home county. He was killed at Ypres at the Battle of Passchendaele during the First World War. Much of Ledwidge's work was published in newspapers and journals in Ireland and the UK. The only work published in book form during his lifetime was the original *Songs of the Fields* (1915).

Michael Longley (1939–) was born in Belfast and educated at Trinity College. He joined the Northern Ireland Arts Council in 1970. His collections of poetry include *No Continuing City: Poems 1963–1968* (1969), *Poems 1963–1983* (1985), *The Echo Gate: Poems 1975–1979* (1979), the acclaimed *Gorse Fires* (1991), *The Ghost Orchid* (1998), *Selected Poems* (1998) and *The Weather in Japan* (2000).

Louis MacNeice (1907–1963) was born in Belfast and educated at the University of Oxford. A poet and playwright, he worked for twenty years as a literary producer at the BBC. His extensive output places him as the major Northern Irish writer of his time.

Derek Mahon (1942–) was born in Belfast and educated at Trinity College. A poet and literary journalist, he is noted for his command of the long poem. His volumes of poetry include *Poems 1962–1978* (1979),

The Hudson Letter (1995), *The Yellow Book* (1997) and *Collected Poems* (1999). He has also translated works from French, including Edmond Rostand's *Cyrano de Bergerac*.

Francis Sylvester Mahony ('Father Prout') (1804–1866) was ordained a priest, but abandoned the church for life as a writer. Born in Cork and educated at the Jesuit Clongowes Wood College, he became a journalist and the author of popular ballads.

James Clarence Mangan (1803–1849), born in Dublin and educated at a Jesuit school, was a journalist and symbolist poet. He adopted many voices to express the anguish of his times. Although his early poetry was often apolitical, after the Great Famine he began writing poems with a strong nationalist bent.

Thomas McCarthy (1954–), poet and novelist, was born in Cappoquin, Co. Waterford and educated at University College Cork. Public, historic and familial themes preoccupy his work. *Seven Winters in Paris* (1989) and *Mr Dineen's Careful Parade: New and Selected Poems* (1999) are two of his volumes of poetry.

Thomas D'Arcy McGee (1825–1868) was born in Carlingford, Co. Louth. He was a journalist and member of the Young Ireland movement. In 1842, aged sixteen, he sailed to the USA, and in the 1850s lived in Canada, where he became active in Canadian politics. He was assassinated because of his opposition to Irish nationalism.

Medbh McGuckian (1950–) was born in Belfast and educated at Queen's University, Belfast. A poet and novelist, she tackles domestic themes, gender and public issues. Collections of her work include *On Ballycastle Beach* (1988), *Marconi's Cottage* (1991) and *Captain Lavender* (1994). In 2002 she was awarded the Forward Poetry Prize for her poem 'She is in the Past, She Has This Grace'.

Brian Merriman (1750–1805) was born in Ennistimon, Co. Clare. He was a farmer and teacher, and is particularly remembered for his long poem in Irish, 'The Midnight Court' (1780), a satire on contemporary sexuality and marriage, which has had a strong influence on the modern-day writings of Seamus Heaney and Thomas Kinsella.

Alice Milligan (1866–1953) was born in Omagh, Co. Tyrone and became a poet and editor. She was active in the Gaelic League, and a central figure of many nationalist bodies as a teacher and organiser. In the 1890s she co-founded two nationalist publications in Northern Ireland.

Ewart Milne (1903–1987), born in Dublin, was a poet and journalist. He published fourteen volumes of poetry, which move from the influence of Yeats to more international modernism. He was awakened politically by the Spanish Civil War, and fought on the republican side. He lived in England between 1942 and 1962.

John Montague (1929–), born in New York, was educated at University College, Dublin.

He is a poet, prose writer and academic, and the first holder of the Ireland Chair of Poetry (1998). A noted commentator on both personal and the public issues, he has published widely, including *The Rough Field* (1972), *The Great Cloak* (1978), *An Occasion of Sin* (1992) and *Collected Poems* (1995).

Thomas Moore (1779–1852) was born in Dublin and educated at Trinity College. He was a poet, singer, songwriter and entertainer, best remembered for his 'Irish Melodies' (1808–34), which popularised Irish culture with Victorian audiences. He was responsible, with John Murray, for burning Lord Byron's memoirs after his death.

Zozimus (Michael Moran) (*c*.1794–1846), born in Dublin, was balladeer, street-singer and reciter of poems. He became blind as an infant, and was noted for his prodigious memory in political and religious recitations. His nickname comes from a popular eighteenth-century poem that he was often called to recite.

Paul Muldoon (1951–) was born in Eglish, Co. Armagh and educated at Queens University, Belfast. A poet, editor and academic, he is noted for his manipulative skill with language and verbal experimentation. His collections of poetry include *Quoof* (1983), *Madoc* (1990) and *The Annals of Chile* (1994). *Moy Sand and Gravel* (2002) won the Pulitzer Prize.

Richard Murphy (1927–), born in Co. Mayo, was brought up in Sri Lanka and Ireland, and educated at the University of

Oxford. Much of his best work is focused on the life and history of the west of Ireland – *Sailing to an Island* (1963), *The Battle of Aughrim* (1968) and *Collected Poems* (2000).

Thomas Newburgh (1695–1779) was born in Dublin, educated at Oxford, and inherited estates in Co. Cavan. He is remembered principally for his *Essays Poetical, Moral and Critical* (1769). His poetry included descriptions of buildings and monuments, which was unusual for the period.

Eiléan Ní Chuilleanáin (1942–) was born in Cork and educated at the University of Oxford. A poet and academic, her work is noted for the evocation of forgotten resonances of people and places. Her poetry collections include *The Rose Geranium* (1991), *Site of Ambush* (1975) and *The Magdalene Sermon* (1990). Her first collection, *Acts and Monuments*, won the Patrick Kavanagh Poetry Award in 1973.

Nuala Ní Dhomhnaill (1952–) was born in Lancashire and spent her childhood in the Gaeltacht of Dingle in County Kerry. She was educated at University College, Cork. Apart from her poetry collections, her works include children's plays, screenplays, anthologies, articles, reviews and essays. Her poems appear in English translation in the dual-language editions *Selected Poems* (1986) and *The Astrakhan Coat* (1992).

Dáibhí Ó Bruadair (1625–1698) was one of the most significant Irish-language poets of the seventeenth century. Born in Barrymore, Co. Cork, he wrote of his despair at the decline of the Gaelic aristocracy and his personal loss of status. His poetry focuses on the political turmoil and dispossessions of the seventeenth century.

Antoine Ó Raifteiri (1779–1835) was born in Killedan, Co. Mayo. He lived a life of poverty and was blinded by smallpox as a child. A poet and wandering minstrel, he made his living by playing his fiddle and performing his songs and poems in the mansions of the Anglo-Irish gentry. His verses in Irish survived in the oral tradition and folklore of south Co. Galway.

Flann O'Brien (Myles na gCopaleen/ Brian O'Nolan/Brian Ó Nualláin) (1911– 1966) was born in Strabane, Co. Tyrone and educated at University College Dublin. He is best known for his novels *At Swim-Two-Birds* (1939) and *The Third Policeman*. His many short columns in the *Irish Times,* under the heading 'Cruiskeen Lawn', established him as a humorous and satirical writer of remarkable inventive powers.

Dermot O'Byrne (Sir Arnold Edward Trevor Bax) (1883–1953) was born in London and educated at the Royal Academy of Music. A composer and latterly Master of the King's Musick, he lived in Dublin from 1910 to 1914, becoming an Irish nationalist and adopting an Irish pseudonym. Known in England as a composer, Bax carried on a separate life as a writer of poetry and drama in Ireland, working under his pseudonym. His 'Ballad' was banned as seditious by the British authorities in Ireland.

John O'Keeffe (1747–1833) was born in Dublin and first studied art before settling on a career as an actor and playwright. He moved to London in 1777. He wrote over sixty plays, including *Tony Lumpkin in Town* (1778) and *Wild Oats* (1791), and was the most produced playwright in London in the last quarter of the eighteenth century. The essayist William Hazlitt described him as 'The English Molière'.

Egan O'Rahilly (*c.*1670–1729) was born in Co. Kerry. His poems in Irish lament the passing of the traditional order of native aristocracy and reflect the hope of a Jacobite victory at the Battle of the Boyne. His best known and most popular poem is 'Gile na Gile' ('Brightness Most Bright').

Seumas O'Sullivan (James Sullivan Starkey) (1879–1958) was born in Dublin and lived there all his life. He was a poet and the editor of the *Dublin Magazine* from 1923 to 1958, using his position to promote younger Irish writers. His books include *Twilight People* (1905), *Collected Poems* (1912), *The Lamplighter* (1929) and *Dublin Poems* (1946).

Bishop Patrick (1047–1084) was Bishop of Dublin. The Latin poem in this anthology was popular in the medieval period, and over a hundred manuscripts of it survive in monastic collections. It is addressed to Bishop Wulfstan, then Abbot of Worcester.

George 'AE' Russell (1867–1935), born in Lurgan, Co. Armagh, studied at the Metropolitan School of Art. He was a painter, poet, mystic, editor and agricultural co-operative organiser – a central figure of Irish cultural life – and his wide range of interests produced a distinguished body of work. He held a literary salon at his home in Rathmines.

Richard Brinsley Sheridan (1751–1816) was born in Dublin. A playwright and politician, he became a major figure in the Westminster parliament for thirty-two years as a Whig, and had great success as a theatre manager and long-time owner of the Theatre Royal, Drury Lane in London. He is known for his comedies, *The Rivals* (1775) and *The School for Scandal* (1777).

James Simmons (1933–2001) was born in Derry and educated at the University of Leeds. A poet and editor, he was the founder of *The Honest Ulsterman* in 1968, and of Poet's House, Islandmagee, in 1989. His work is strongly influenced by the vernacular and ballad forms. His poetry collections include *Poems, 1956–1986*.

Oliver St John Gogarty (1878–1957), born in Dublin, was a surgeon, poet and prose writer, and senator in the Irish Free State. He is mostly remembered as the fictional character Buck Milligan in Joyce's *Ulysses*. He maintained close friendships with W.B. Yeats, AE Russell, Lord Dunsany and other Dublin literati, and was a noted conversationalist and wit.

Jonathan Swift (1667–1745) was born in Dublin and educated at Trinity College. In 1697 he was ordained in the Church of Ireland, and later became Dean of St Patrick's Cathedral, Dublin. Amongst the greatest satirists and political pamphleteers of his time, his major works are *Drapier's Letters* (1724–5), *Gulliver's Travels* (1726) and *A Modest Proposal* (1729).

J.M. Synge (1871–1909) was born in Dublin and educated at Trinity College. He was a composer, poet and playwright, and the author of a number of the most important plays of the Literary Revival. *The Shadow of the Glen* (1903) and *Riders to the Sea* (1904) were plays based on stories Synge had collected on the Aran Islands. *The Playboy of the Western World* (1907), widely regarded as his masterpiece, was first performed at Dublin's Abbey Theatre.

Nahum Tate (1652–1715) was born in Dublin and educated at Trinity College. A poet and dramatist, he adapted and rewrote many of Shakespeare's plays (often giving them happy endings), translated classical authors and produced a new version of the Psalms. He was appointed English Poet Laureate in 1692.

Katharine Tynan (1861–1931), born in Co. Dublin, was a poet, novelist and journalist who played a major part in Dublin's literary circles. She was an important figure of the Literary Revival and a close associate of W.B. Yeats. Remarkably prolific, she published over a hundred novels and five volumes of autobiography; her *Collected Poems* appeared in 1930.

Luke Wadding (1588–1657), born at Waterford, was a Franciscan friar and historian. He was educated in Waterford and Kilkenny and went on to study in Lisbon and at University of Coimbra, Portugal. He was an enthusiastic supporter of the Irish Catholics in the war of 1641, and his college became the strongest advocate of the Irish cause in Rome. Through Wadding's efforts, St Patrick's Day became a feast day. He was a voluminous writer, publishing a total of thirty-six volumes.

Oscar Wilde (1856–1900) was born in Dublin and educated at Trinity College. A writer of enduring influence, he excelled as novelist, playwright and poet. *The Picture of Dorian Gray* (1889), *The Importance of Being Earnest* (1895), and 'The Ballad of Reading Gaol' (1898) are his major works. Convicted of homosexuality in 1895, he died shortly after his release from jail in Paris, aged forty-six.

Macdara Woods (1942–) was born in Dublin and educated at University College Dublin. He is a poet and editor, and his extensive travels have produced a cosmopolitan body of work, including *Selected Poems* (1996) and *Knowledge in the Blood: New and Selected Poems* (2000).

W.B. Yeats (1865–1939), poet and playwright, was born in Dublin and studied at the Metropolitan School of Art. One of the most influential poets of his age and a leading figure of the Literary Revival, he received the 1923 Nobel Prize for Literature. Yeats' spirituality and cultural nationalism became vehicles for some of the most memorable poetry in Irish literature.

Artists' Biographies

Francis Bacon (1909–1992) was born in Dublin, and left home at sixteen to live with an uncle in Berlin. In 1928 he moved to Paris, where he decided to become an artist after seeing an exhibition of Picasso's work. He became one of the most distinguished figurative artists of the twentieth century, celebrated for his visceral paintings of human figures. Following his death his famously chaotic London studio was reconstructed in Dublin at Dublin City Gallery The Hugh Lane, now a major centre for Bacon studies.

James Barry (1741–1806) was born in Water Lane, Cork. Largely a self-taught artist, in 1763 he attracted the patronage of his Irish compatriot Edmund Burke, who funded Barry to travel to Italy to study. His major work, 'The Progress of Human Culture', is a series of six monumental paintings of historical and allegorical subjects created for the Great Room of the Royal Society of Arts in London.

William Gerard Barry (1864–1941) was born in Ballyadam, Carrigtwohill, Co. Cork, and studied at Cork's Crawford School of Art and at the Académie Julian in Paris. Following an argument with his father, he travelled to Canada and the United States, where he took painting commissions, including, it is said, one to paint President Wilson. He eventually returned to Europe, working from a studio on the French Riviera.

Rose Maynard Barton (1856–1929) is one of Ireland's best-loved watercolour painters, a contemporary of Mildred Anne Butler and Percy French and cousin of Edith Somerville. She began exhibiting her broad-wash watercolour paintings with the Watercolour Society of Ireland in 1872, and in 1875 visited Brussels to study under the French artist, Henri Gervex. Her paintings can be seen in public collections including the National Gallery of Ireland and Dublin City Gallery The Hugh Lane in Dublin, and the Ulster Museum in Belfast.

Robert Bottom (1944–) was born in Cambridge, England and trained at Canterbury College of Art. He was Head of Art at Campbell College, Belfast from 1975 to 1995, and now paints full time, mostly landscapes and seascapes. His paintings are in public collections including those of Allied Irish Bank and Belfast City Council.

Alicia Boyle (1908–1997) was born of Irish parents in Bangkok, Siam, and brought up in Ulster and London. She studied at the Byam Shaw School of Drawing and Painting, then worked in Greece and England; her first solo exhibition was held in the Peter Jones Gallery, London, in 1945. In 1971 she moved to a purpose-built studio near Bantry, exhibiting widely in Ireland. A major retrospective was held at the Arts Council Gallery in 1983.

Brian Bourke (1936–) was born in Dublin and studied at the National College of Art & Design in Dublin and St Martin's School of Art in London. In 1965 he represented Ireland at both the Paris Biennale and the Lugano Exhibition of Graphics. He won the Arts Council portrait competition in 1965, the Munster and Leinster Bank competition in 1966, and first prize in the Irish Exhibition of Living Art competition in 1967. In 1985, he was named Sunday Independent Artist of the Year, and received the O'Malley Award from the Irish-American Cultural Institute in 1993. Major exhibitions of his work were shown at IMMA and the RHA. His work has been exhibited across Europe and the USA, and in 1991 he was artist-in-residence at the Gate Theatre's Beckett Festival in Dublin, with accompanying works appearing at the Douglas Hyde Gallery.

Muriel Brandt (1909–1981) studied at the Belfast College of Art and at the Royal College of Art in London, where she was elected Associate Royal College of Art in 1937. As well as working in oil and watercolours, she painted mural decorations, portraits and landscapes, and was commissioned to paint the portraits of many Dublin notables, among them Sir Alfred Chester Beatty. She also painted the panels in the Franciscan church of Adam and Eve on Merchant's Quay, Dublin.

Frederick William Burton (1816–1900) was born in Corofin, Co. Clare. In 1842 he began to exhibit at the Royal Academy, and a visit to Germany and Bavaria that year was the first of many European travels. His best-known paintings, 'The Aran Fisherman's Drowned Child' (1841) and 'The Meeting on the Turret Stairs' (1864), are exhibited at the National Gallery of Ireland.

Mildred Anne Butler (1858–1941), born in Thomastown, Co. Kilkenny, travelled to Brussels and Paris in the early 1880s, studying alongside Walter Osborne and John Lavery. Her works were exhibited in the USA and Japan, and the Kilkenny Museum of Art was renamed The Butler Gallery in her honour.

Frederick Calvert (1793–1852) was born in Cork. Although better known for his coastal shipping scenes, in the early part of his career he concentrated on landscape painting. His first exhibited work was a 'View near Rathfarnham' in the 1812 exhibition of the Society of Artists of Ireland in Dublin. He moved to London in 1827, and it was at the 1837 Belfast Association of Artists exhibition that he first showed two marine scenes.

Arthur Campbell (1909–1994) was born in Belfast, though he spent his first nine years in Dublin and Arklow, Co. Wicklow. An artist and photographer, he was one of a family of artists which included his brother George and his mother Gretta Bowen. Although he took life drawing night-classes at the Art College in Belfast, Campbell was mainly self-taught. His photographs were published in *The Observer*, *Photography*, *The Irish Times* and other journals, and he helped illustrate several books. Several of his paintings are in the collection of the Ulster Museum.

George Campbell (1917–1979) was born in Arklow, Co. Wicklow, brother of Arthur and son of the painter Gretta Bowen, but grew up in the city of Belfast. Mainly self-taught, he began to paint during the Second World War. Campbell was one of a group of Belfast artists, including Gerard Dillon and Daniel O'Neill, who brought a new progressive sense of purpose to the Dublin art scene in the 1940s.

Betty Christie (1952–) was born in Limavady, Co. Derry, and spent her childhood in the countryside. She has lived in Belfast for over forty years, but her work is still influenced by her rural upbringing. She graduated from the Belfast College of Art and Design in 1975. Her work is representational, mainly in pastel or in watercolour, with some mixed media.

David Clarke (1920–2006) was born into a family of artists and studied under Mainie Jellett. His father, Harry Clarke, was the renowned stained glass artist and book illustrator, and his mother was the painter Margaret Clarke. Clarke was a fine draughtsman but he was primarily a colourist, inducing peace or excitement through cool or glowing colours.

Harry Clarke (1889–1931), the son of a Dublin stained-glass supplier, benefited from the rebirth of stained glass as an art form at Sarah Purser's An Túr Gloine studios. During his short life he created over 160 stained-glass windows for religious and commercial commissions throughout England and Ireland and further afield. His works include the controversial Geneva Window commissioned by the Irish Free State, illustrating Irish writers and artists.

Patrick Collins (1911–1994) was born in Dromana West, Co. Sligo. He studied life drawing under George Collie, and in 1945 became a full-time painter, living in a tower in the grounds of Howth Castle, which became a gathering place for artists and writers. He first exhibited in the Irish Exhibition of Living Art in 1950. In 1971 Collins moved to France, but six years later returned to Ireland to live in Delgany.

William Conor (1881–1968) entered the Belfast Government School of Design at thirteen to be trained in drawing for industry. He is noted for his sympathetic genre-paintings of working-class life, and his paintings were popular and widely shown during his lifetime. A champion of the ordinary woman, for Conor the Irish shawl came to represent their determined spirit.

Charles Henry Cook (*c*.1830– *c*.1906) was born in Bandon, Co. Cork. He was a genre painter, mainly of scenes of Irish life and landscapes, living with his mother at Sunday's Well in Cork, where he also worked. He moved to Bath, England, in around 1870.

Barrie Cooke (1931–) has lived for many years in Ireland, but was born in Cheshire and spent his childhood in England, the United States, Jamaica and Bermuda. An early enthusiasm for marine biology took him to Harvard University, but shortly after enrolling he switched to art history. He studied art at Skowhegan in Maine and exhibited in Boston in the 1950s before deciding to settle in Co. Clare. He is a keen fisherman and naturalist.

Vicki Crowley (1940–) was born in Malta, and was educated there and in England. Her husband is Irish, and in 1970 she returned with her family to Ireland where she established a studio in Barna from where she works.

Francis Danby (1793–1861) was born in Killinick, Co. Wexford, and moved with his family to Dublin during the 1798 Wexford Rising. He studied painting at the Royal Dublin Society art schools, specialising in landscape painting. In 1819 he met the Reverend John Eagles who encouraged him to seek inspiration for his paintings in the local scenery. By the 1820s, however, Danby abandoned naturalism in favour of poetic and heroic landscapes inspired by Claude and Turner.

Lilian Lucy Davidson (1893–1954) was born in Bray, Co. Wicklow. She studied at the National College of Art and Design, and began exhibiting with the Water Colour Society of Ireland when she was nineteen. In 1914 she met Mainie Jellet, with whom she held a joint exhibition in 1920 at her studio in Earlsfort Terrace, Dublin. Among her portrait subjects were Jack B. Yeats, Sarah Purser, George 'AE' Russell, Austin Clarke and Joseph Holloway.

Gerard Dillon (1916–1971) was born in Belfast, the youngest of eight children. He left school at fourteen to be apprenticed to a painting and decorating firm. A visit to Connemara in 1939 provided inspiration for his painting, and in 1943 he exhibited with Daniel O'Neill at the Contemporary Picture Galleries, Dublin. He was among a group of Irish artists who showed in 1947 at the Associated American Artists' galleries in New York. In 1958 Dillon was one of the artists chosen to represent Britain in the Pittsburgh International Exhibition of Contemporary Art.

Lady Kate Dobbin (1868–1955) was born in Bristol, England, the daughter of a solicitor. She moved to Cork in 1887 where she married Alfred Graham Dobbin, the city's High Sheriff, and owner of the Imperial Hotel. From 1891 to 1895 Lady Dobbin studied drawing and painting at the Crawford Municipal School of Art. In 1894 she submitted a work to the Royal Hibernian Academy's Annual Exhibition in Dublin, the first of more than a hundred contributions to the RHA.

Anna Marie Dowdican (1969–) was born in Co. Donegal. She moved to Sligo where she studied fine art for four years, and now lives there. Dowdican has had fourteen solo exhibitions, and her work has been exhibited nationally and internationally. In 1998 she published Imagine, a collection of poetry and photography, and in 2002 Paint Me, with selected paintings, drawings and essays, was published by the Black Battler Press.

Martin Driscoll (1945–) was born in the USA but spent most summer vacations in Ireland. He has dual citizenship due to his Irish-born parents and now splits his time between Co. Kerry and Texas. He studied under Frank Reilly. Driscoll's pastoral scenes of rural Irish life have received much critical acclaim.

Patrick Vincent Duffy (1832–1909) was the son of a silversmith and jeweller. He received his art education in the school of the Royal Dublin Society, and began to exhibit at the Royal Hibernian Academy in 1851. He became a full member just a few months later and was appointed Keeper of the RHA in 1870, a post he held for thirty-eight years.

Beatrice Elvery (Beatrice Glenavy) (1881–1970), the daughter of a Dublin silk merchant, studied at the Dublin Metropolitan School of Art under William Orpen, who used her as a model and remained her lifelong friend and correspondent. She joined Sarah Purser's studio An Túr Gloine in 1903 and her first commission of six windows was installed in the Convent of Mercy in Enniskillen. She married Charles Campbell, Second Baron Glenavy, and the couple moved in the highest literary circles including Yeats, Shaw and D.H. Lawrence.

Michael Farrell (1940–2000) was born in Kells, Co. Meath, and studied at St Martin's School of Art, London, and at Colchester College of Art. In 1971 he settled in Paris. His distinctive style, combining hard-edge pattern and figurative references in a soft-sprayed background, dates from 1965, when he consciously introduced Celtic motifs. During the 1990s he renewed his obsession with Joyce in the 'La Rencontre' canvases (1994).

Trevor Fowler (1800–*c*.1844), a portrait painter, was born in Dublin. He exhibited at the Royal Hibernian Academy in Dublin between 1830 and 1835, and at the National Academy in New York in 1838. From 1841 he worked in New Orleans. In 1843 he studied in Paris, returning to New Orleans in 1844.

William Percy French (1854–1920) was born at Cloonyquin, Co. Roscommon, the second son of landowner Christopher French and his wife Susan Emma (née Percy). Known to his family and friends as 'Willie', he entered Trinity College, Dublin in 1872 to study civil engineering. Here, instead of focusing on his academic studies, he developed his talents for songwriting, dramatics, banjo playing and watercolour painting. He was one of Ireland's foremost songwriters and entertainers in his day, and has only recently become recognised for his watercolour paintings.

Hugh Douglas Hamilton (*c*.1734–1808) was born in Dublin. He studied art under Robert West at the Dublin Society House, concentrating on crayon and pastels in his early career. He lived in London in the early 1760s, where he was often overwhelmed with orders, including his portraits of the British royal family such as Queen Charlotte (1746). Following the advice of fellow artist John Flaxman, Hamilton turned to oil paintings, later painting the portraits of many of Ireland's prominent historical figures of the period including his portrait of Dean Kirwan, which is displayed at the Royal Dublin Society.

Grace Henry (1863–1953), the second of ten children of a Church of Scotland minister, studied drawing and painting in Paris where she met her husband-to-be, Paul Henry. In 1910 a holiday on Achill Island, off the Mayo coast, prompted a move to the west of Ireland in 1912. Grace eventually separated from Henry, who omitted all reference to her in his two-volume autobiography. In her later years Grace Henry travelled extensively; it is largely due to her nomadic lifestyle that many of her paintings have not survived.

Paul Henry (1876–1958) attended the Belfast School of Art, after which a family member financed a trip to Paris in 1889, where he studied and met his wife Grace. In 1912 they moved to Achill Island, where Henry discovered his true post-impressionist style. In 1919 he and Grace moved to Dublin where, with other painters including Jack B. Yeats and Mary Swanzy, they founded the Society of Dublin Painters. During the 1920s several of Henry's works were reproduced as posters and prints, helping to establish the standard scenic view of Ireland.

Evie Hone (1894–1955), Dublin-born painter and stained glass artist, was related to the two Nathaniel Hones. Her most important works are the east window of the chapel at Eton College, Windsor, and 'My Four Green Fields', commissioned for the Irish government's pavilion at the 1939 New York World's Fair. Like her companion Mainie Jellett, Hone studied under Walter Sickert in London and André Lhote and Albert Gleizes in Paris. She worked as a member of the An Túr Gloine stained glass co-operative before setting up a studio of her own in Rathfarnham.

Charles Jervas (Jarvis) (*c*.1675–1739) was a popular portrait painter, translator, and art collector. He lived most of his adult life in England. An apprentice to the painter Sir Godfrey Kneller, he later studied drawing in Rome and then returned to England. Succeeding Kneller, he became court painter to the English kings George I and George II.

Sean Keating (1889–1977) was born in Limerick and studied drawing at the Limerick Technical School before winning a scholarship, arranged by William Orpen, to study fine art painting. Over the next few years he spent time on the Aran Islands and then in London, at Orpen's studio. In 1916 he returned to Ireland where he documented the War of Independence and the subsequent Civil War. He held conservative views on art and exerted an influence against modern art in Ireland, being a committed defender of traditional painting.

Harry Kernoff (1900–1974) was born in London and then moved to Dublin. He became a leading figure in Irish modernism. Kernoff is famously associated with Davy Byrne's pub in Dublin, where he was a close friend with the original owner. His 'Oliver

St John Gogarty' is the portrait of a surgeon, wit and writer, a friend of James Joyce who described him in *Ulysses* as 'a stately plump buck Mulligan'. When Gogarty's house burnt down in the 1920s he reopened it as a hotel, now Renvyle House Hotel, which he ran on eccentric lines, including W.B. Yeats amongst its guests.

Henry Wright Kerr (1857–1936) was born in Edinburgh, and worked extensively in both Ireland and Scotland. He worked in watercolour, illustrating many books such as The Lighter Side of Irish Life and Reminiscences of Scottish Life and Character. He studied at the Life School of the Royal Scottish Academy, and though he mostly painted genre scenes of Scottish and Irish characters, after 1900 he increasingly worked in portraiture.

Tom Kerr (1925–) was born in Holywood, Co. Down, and has lived there most of his life. Kerr is also known for the success of the Kerr Art Group, a select coterie of painters in North Down, which meets regularly to work under his guidance. Over decades the Group, through its exhibitions and the sale of members' paintings, has raised many thousands of pounds for the good causes it supports.

Richard King (1907–1974) was an Irish stained glass artist and illustrator. He was born in Castlebar, Co. Mayo, where his father was a sergeant in the Royal Irish Constabulary. In 1926 he became a student at the Dublin Metropolitan School of Art and in 1928 he entered the stained glass

studio of Harry Clarke. When Clarke died in early 1931, King completed the ongoing work on the windows of St Mel's Cathedral in Longford, and managed the studio from 1935 to 1940. He then worked independently from his own studio in Dalkey. Between 1933 and 1949 he also designed twelve Irish stamps.

Charles Vincent Lamb (1893–1964), born in Portadown, Co. Armagh, attended evening classes at the Belfast College of Art whilst working for the family business by day. A scholarship enabled him to go to Dublin in 1917 to study at the College of Art, where he won gold and silver medals.

John Lavery (1856–1941), born in Belfast, attended the Haldane Academy in Glasgow and the Académie Julian in Paris. In 1888 he was commissioned to paint the state visit of Queen Victoria to the Glasgow International Exhibition, which launched his career as a society painter. In 1909 Lavery married Hazel Martyn, an Irish-American known for her beauty and poise, who figures in more than four hundred of her husband's paintings. Hazel modelled for her husband's allegorical figure of Ireland, reproduced on Irish banknotes from 1928 to 1975. Lavery was appointed an official war artist in 1914, but ill health prevented him from travelling to France; he remained in Britain and painted the war effort on the home front. After the war Lavery and his wife became interested in their Irish heritage, offering the use of their London home to the Irish negotiators during the Treaty negotiations.

Luke Lawnicki (1966–) was born in Poland and studied at the University of Education in Krakow. He moved to Ireland in 2001 and lives in Co. Waterford. He exhibits with selected galleries both nationally and internationally, and his artworks are held in many private collections in Ireland, Germany and Poland.

Louis le Brocquy (1916–) has received many accolades in a career that spans seventy years. Born in Dublin, the artist is widely acknowledged for his evocative portraits of literary figures and fellow artists including his friends Samuel Beckett, Francis Bacon and W.B. Yeats, whom he knew as a young boy. His work is represented in numerous public collections from the Guggenheim to the Tate. In Ireland he is honoured as the first and only living painter to be included in the Permanent Irish Collection of the National Gallery.

Patrick Leonard (1918–2005) was born in Co. Dublin. He studied fine art painting and figure drawing under Sean Keating and Maurice MacGonigal at the Metropolitan School of Art, Dublin, and started exhibiting at the Royal Hibernian Academy in 1941. From 1953 to 1982 Leonard was a full-time art teacher in Dublin. Bouts of illness often interrupted his work, but although he would stop painting during these periods he continued sketching and drawing. These sketches were later worked into finished oil paintings. Leonard's realist genre-painting featured the small scenes of everyday life. He had a one-man exhibition at the Oriel

Gallery in Dublin, in 1979, and a substantial retrospective in 1990 at the Gorry Gallery.

Daniel MacDonald (1821–1853) was born in Cork, son of a local painter James McDaniel. Taught drawing at an early age by his father, MacDonald soon demonstrated his sketching skills, becoming noted for his pen and ink drawings. In his early twenties he began exhibiting at the Royal Hibernian Academy, before leaving for London. MacDonald is one of the few Irish artists of the nineteenth century to depict country people without excessive sentimentalising or idealising. His works can be seen in the National Gallery of Ireland in Dublin and the Crawford Gallery in Cork. He also painted one of the only canvases to depict the Famine in Ireland, 'The Irish Peasant Family Discovering the Blight of their Store', exhibited in London in 1847.

Maurice MacGonigal (1900–1979), a talented artist, was famously arrested for his active membership of the Irish Republican Army in December 1920. His illustrations from his period of internment, first at Kilmainham Gaol then at Ballykinlar Internment Camp, provide a unique record of the horrors of this period of Irish history. 'A Republican Execution' is possibly a study for MacGonigal's drawing, 'Death in the Mountains', which won a bronze medal when exhibited at the Tailteann Games in 1928. The firing squad depicted are most likely the RIC auxiliaries, the 'Black and Tans', wearing mismatching parts of borrowed uniforms, whilst a captured priest kneels before an outhouse, minutes before being executed. Released at the Truce, MacGonigal returned to the family stained glass business of his cousin Harry Clarke, where he became a junior partner.

Daniel Maclise (1806–1870) was born in Cork. He was one of the first students to attend the Cork School of Art with fellow students John Hogan and Samuel Forde. In 1827 he moved to London where he attended The Royal Academy Schools. During his early years he supported himself by making pencil portraits, and in 1830 he began his famous series of character portraits for *Frazer's Magazine*. Between 1858 and 1864 he painted a series of large-scale frescoes for the new Houses of Parliament in London. Maclise was attracted to literary and historical subjects; his large painting of 'The Wedding Feast of Aoife and Strongbow' is on view in the National Gallery of Ireland.

Brian Maguire (1951–) is one of a group of contemporary Irish artists who came to the fore in the mid-1980s and whose work can be loosely described as New Expressionist. He was born in Dublin in 1951, and studied at the National College of Art and Design. A growing political involvement with the left-wing Workers' Party interrupted his college years. For many years he has taught art in Irish prisons, and since 1987 has served as artist-in-residence in jails in Limerick, Portlaoise, Dublin, Spike Island in Cork and Masqui Prison in Vancouver. In 1990 he was awarded the O'Malley Art Award by the Irish American Cultural Institute.

Emmet McNamara (1976–) was born in Dublin. His interest in painting and drawing started as a young boy. From drawing buses and city life, he has moved on to more Irish themes. He has also illustrated a number of picture books for children.

Joseph McWilliams (1938–) was born in Belfast, and studied at the Belfast College of Art. He taught at the Ulster Polytechnic and the University of Ulster. In 1986 he opened the Cavehill Gallery, and in 1988 was awarded the silver medal at the Royal Ulster Academy exhibition. He is well known for his vibrant and energetic depiction of community and political life in Belfast, particularly loyalist and nationalist parades.

Charlotte Mangan (1978–) was born in Limerick and grew up in Co. Clare. She began painting at an early age. She studied at University College Dublin and Roma Tre University in Italy. She lives in Dublin.

Colin Middleton (1910–1983) was born in Belfast, and trained at Belfast College of Art. Heavily influenced by the work of Vincent van Gogh, he regarded himself as the only surrealist working in Ireland in the 1930s. His work first appeared at the Royal Hibernian Academy in 1938 and was followed by his first solo exhibition at the Grafton Gallery in 1944. A damask-designer like his father, he now devoted himself to full-time painting. In 1953 he moved to Bangor, where he designed for the New

Theatre. In 1954 he started his career as an art teacher at the Belfast College of Art and at Coleraine Technical School, eventually becoming Head of Art at Friends' School, Lisburn.

Carmel Mooney (1962–) was born in Kilkenny, and lives and works in Dublin. She studied at the National College of Art and Design. She held her first solo exhibition at the Lincoln Gallery, Dublin, in 1983. A lecturer in the History of Painting, she was also Artistic Director at Daon Scoil, An Daingean, from 1981 to 1991. A visit to Lanzarote in 1990 introduced her to its volcanic landscape, and she returned many times to work there.

Richard Thomas Moynan (1856–1906) was born in Dublin and studied there at the Metropolitan School. He originally set out to study medicine, but opted for a career in the arts shortly before his final examinations. He enrolled at the Dublin Metropolitan School of Art in 1879 and won both the Taylor and Cowper (awarded to the best drawing from life) competitions. In 1883 he attended the Academy in Antwerp along with Roderic O'Conor and Henry Allen. He studied there until moving to Paris in 1885. By the late 1880s Moynan had returned to Dublin to exhibit his paintings, becoming a member of the Royal Hibernian Academy in 1890.

Mick Mulcahy (1952–), born in Co. Cork, is an Irish expressionist painter who lives and works in Paris, but returns frequently to Ireland. He was educated at the Crawford Municipal School of Art in Cork and the National College of Art and Design in Dublin. He has travelled extensively, particularly in north and west Africa, where he has lived and worked in the local community. In 1994 the Douglas Hyde Gallery in Dublin held a major exhibition of his work.

William Mulready (1786–1863), born in Ennis, Co. Clare, is best known for his romanticising depictions of rural scenes. In 1792 his family moved to London, where he was educated and was taught painting well enough to be accepted at the Royal Academy School at the age of fourteen. Many of his early pictures are landscapes, but from 1808 on he started to build a reputation as a genre painter, painting mostly everyday scenes from rural life. In 1802 he married Elizabeth Varley, a landscape painter, and their three children, Paul Augustus, William, and Michael also became artists.

Erskine Nicol (1825–1904) was born in Leith, Scotland. A student of William Allan, he taught in Dublin, Ireland, from 1845 to 1850, at the height of the Irish famine, and identified with the oppression of the Irish people, and much of his work portrays the injustices inflicted upon the Irish population during the nineteenth century.

Andrew Nicholl (1804–1886), son of a bootmaker and younger brother of painter William Nicholl, was an apprentice in F.D. Finlay's printing shop and worked as a compositor on the newly established *Northern Whig*. In 1836 he became a founder member of the Belfast Association of Artists and exhibited at the Royal Hibernian Academy in Dublin (which elected him as a member in 1848) and the Royal Academy, London, as well as in his native city. He contributed drawings to the *Dublin Penny Journal*, as well as to the series *Views of the Dublin and Kingstown Railway*.

Geraldine M. O'Brien (1922–) was born in Limerick into a distinguished artistic family. Her mother, Cicely O'Brien, was a well-known artist and her cousin was the renowned Dermod O'Brien, president of the Royal Hibernian Academy. O'Brien showed her talent while still at school in Dublin, twice winning prizes at the Royal Drawing Society. In 1939 she went to study for a year with the Dublin-born artist Stanhope Alexander Forbes in Cornwall. She is best known as a flower painter.

Diarmuid O'Ceallachain (1915–1993) was born in Cork and studied at the Crawford School of Art. In 1939 he received the coveted Taylor Prize for his painting 'The Struggle', and won several later awards including the Académie Française Prix Thorlet in 1958. In 1991 the Crawford Municipal Art Gallery hosted a major retrospective exhibition.

Aloysius O'Kelly (1853–*c.*1941) was born to a blacksmith father but his mother guided him to a life in art, sending him to London to study sculpture. His drawings in the

London Illustrated News portrayed the unrest in 1880s Ireland, where his brother had been jailed for political activities. O'Kelly lived and painted rural scenes in Concarneau and Connemara, before moving to New York.

John O'Leary (1929–1999) was born in Cork and studied at the Crawford School of Art. He was awarded the Gibson Bequest Scholarship to study in Paris, where he attended the Atelier André Lhote and the Académie Julian. A founding member of Cork Arts Society, O'Leary's work has featured in exhibitions nationwide and was the subject of a retrospective at the Crawford Art Gallery in 2002.

Tony O'Malley (1913–2003) was born in Callan, Co. Kilkenny. He was a self-taught artist, having started painting while recovering from tuberculosis in the 1940s. He resumed his banking career in the 1950s but retired in 1959. In 1960 he went to live in St Ives in Cornwall and stayed for thirty years, later visiting Ireland during the summers. His early work is figurative, but his interest in expressing inner worlds and the influence of St Ives later led him towards abstraction.

Frank O'Meara (1853–1888) was born in Carlow, the son of a doctor. In 1875 he visited the artists' colonies in Barbizon and Grez-sur-Loing, where John Lavery and Carl Larsson were among his peers. He settled there and eventually befriended Robert Louis Stevenson. In the spring of 1888 he returned to Carlow, where he died either from malaria fever or tuberculosis. Though his output was small, it is easily recognised by its melancholy, autumnal mood and use of subdued but harmonious tones. Five of his works hang at The Hugh Lane Gallery of Modern Art in Dublin.

Daniel O'Neill (1920–1974) was born in Belfast. The son of an electrician, and himself an electrician by trade, he was largely self-taught, although he briefly attended Belfast College of Art life classes, before working with and studying under Sidney Smith. The advent of his painting career coincided with the outbreak of World War II. His first exhibition was in 1941 at the Mol Gallery, Belfast. Within five years the Dublin art dealer Victor Waddington had taken him in hand, granting a regular income, which allowed him to give up his day job. In the early 1950s O'Neill left Belfast, moving to the village of Conlig, Co. Down, which had a small-scale artist's colony at the time, with George Campbell and Gerard Dillon. He returned to Belfast in 1971.

William Orpen (1878–1931), born in Stillorgan, Co. Dublin, was a fine draughtsman and popular portrait painter in the period leading up to the First World War. Although his studio was in London, he was much involved in the Celtic revival in his native Ireland, and spent time in Ireland painting, befriending Hugh Lane. Like Lavery, Orpen was an official war painter of the First World War, where on the Western Front he produced harrowing drawings and paintings of dead soldiers and German prisoners of war.

Walter Frederick Osborne (1859–1903) was born in Rathmines, Dublin, the son of a successful animal painter. In 1881 and 1882, while studying in Antwerp, he won the Taylor Prize, the highest student honour in Ireland of the time. After working in Europe, in the 1880s he moved to England where he painted alongside Nathaniel Hill and Augustus Burke at Walberswick. In 1892 he returned to Ireland to paint portraits and Dublin scenes in the Impressionist style.

George Petrie (1790–1866) was born in Dublin, the son of the portrait and miniature painter James Petrie. He was interested in art from an early age and was sent to the Dublin Society's Schools, where he was educated as an artist and won the silver medal in 1805. He produced sketches for engravings for travel books including Thomas Cromwell's *Excursions through Ireland*, and James Norris Brewer's *Beauties of Ireland*. His favourite medium was watercolour which, due to the prejudices of the age, was considered inferior to oil painting. Some of his best work is in the collections of the National Gallery of Ireland.

Sarah Purser (1848–1943) was born in Dun Laoghaire, one of eleven children. When her father's grain and milling business failed and he emigrated to America, she moved to Dublin with her mother. After studying in Paris, she returned to Dublin in the 1880s and set about earning a living from painting portraits. Her talent, as well as her sociability and her friendship with the influential Gore-Booths, meant she obtained a large number of portrait commissions. Her other portrait subjects included W.B. Yeats and his brother Jack. A sparkling hostess, she became very wealthy through astute investments, especially in Guinness. Throughout her long life she was active in the Irish art world, being instrumental in the establishment of the Hugh Lane Municipal Gallery of Modern Art.

Nano Reid (1905–1981) trained at the Metropolitan School of Art in Dublin, where she studied under Sean Keating and Harry Clarke. She then travelled to Paris, enrolling at the Grand Chaumiere. Following her studies in Paris, Reid attended the Central School in London, studying under Bernard Meninsky. Her first solo exhibition was held at the Dublin Painters Gallery in 1934. After returning to Ireland, Reid spent the rest of her life in Drogheda, concentrating on painting aspects of local life and landscapes. In 1950, along with Norah McGuinness, Reid represented Ireland at the Venice Biennale.

Markey Robinson (1917–1999) was a prolific artist with a distinctive naïve expressionist style. His main passion was painting, but he also produced sculptures, and designed some stained glass panels. The son of a house painter, he spent time as a boxer and as a merchant sailor. His first exhibitions were in Belfast during World War II, but he became better known through his exhibitions at the Oriel Gallery in Dublin where over twenty exhibitions were held. His paintings cover a wide range of subjects, but there are certain recurring features, for example women wearing dark shawls with no facial features visible.

George 'AE' Russell (1867–1935) was born in Co. Armagh and brought up in Dublin. He studied drawing and painting at evening classes at the Metropolitan School of Art and attended evening classes at the Royal Hibernian Academy. In his spare time, encouraged by his friend W.B. Yeats, he wrote poetry, studied theosophy and painted murals. Russell became an officer of the Irish Agricultural Organization Society, an agricultural co-operative movement, and travelled extensively throughout Ireland as its spokesman. In 1903 he exhibited over forty paintings in Dublin, and more exhibitions followed, both solo and with Constance Gore-Booth. Between 1907 and 1911 he took part in group exhibitions with artists such as William Leech and Dermod O'Brien, and continued painting, exhibiting and lecturing up until his death.

Robert Ryan (1964–) was born in Limerick. He graduated from Limerick School of Art And Design in 1987 and went on to work in London and Copenhagen before returning to Ireland in 1994. He has travelled extensively in Europe, Africa, Asia, America and most recently Australia. Ryan has had many solo shows and has regularly shown in major annual exhibitions.

Patrick Scott (1921–) lives and works in Dublin. He studied architecture at University College Dublin and went on to practise as an architect in the office of Michael Scott from 1945 to 1960, when he began to paint full time. He is also well known for his tapestries, having collaborated with the V'soske Joyce carpet company in Co. Galway, developing new tapestry techniques. He has had two major retrospective exhibitions – in 1981 at the Douglas Hyde Gallery, Dublin; Ulster Museum, Belfast; and the Crawford Gallery, Cork; and in 2002 at the Hugh Lane and Crawford Galleries.

Mary Swanzy (1882–1978), born in Merrion Square, Dublin, is considered to be the first Irish Cubist. Early in her career, she was tutored by the painter John Butler Yeats, who encouraged her to undertake further art study in Paris, where she was highly influenced by Cubism. A regular at Gertrude Stein's soirées, she was exposed to work by Picasso and Cézanne.

J.B. Vallely (1941–), a painter and musician, was born into a Co. Armagh family. He sold his first painting in 1958 and then went on to study at the Belfast College of Art from 1959, where he was taught by Tom Carr, and later at the Edinburgh Art College. In 1968 *The Irish Times* regarded him as 'one of the more exciting Irish painters under the age of thirty'. He has had thirty-eight solo exhibitions and is a contributor to many major art collections. In 2000 a retrospective of J.B. Vallely's work was held in Armagh.

Francis Sylvester Walker (1848–1916) was the son of the Master of the Workhouse at Dunshaughlin in Co. Meath. A painter, illustrator and etcher, he studied art at both the Royal Dublin Society and the Royal Hibernian Academy. Known for his landscapes, portraits and genre works, at the turn of the century he also illustrated travel books. His works are currently exhibited in the National Gallery of Ireland in Dublin, the British Museum, and the Victoria and Albert Museum.

Patrick Walshe (1952–) was born in the west of Ireland. He left Dublin to practise his art in New York and Los Angeles in the 1980s where he exhibited widely, returning to Ireland with his family in the 1990s. He now lives in the mountains of Co. Wicklow, south of Dublin.

Robert Lucius West (1774–1850) was born into an artistic dynasty. His grandfather was the founder of the Dublin Society Drawing School, while his father was a draughtsman and accomplished classical scholar. Both men held the position of Master of the Royal Dublin Society Figure School, a position to which Robert Lucius West was appointed in 1809, and which he held until 1845. He exhibited many times with the Society of Artists, and in several other venues in Dublin from 1800 to 1820. He taught at

the Dublin Society Drawing School and in 1809, soon after the death of his father, he was chosen to succeed him as Master. In 1823, on the foundation of the Royal Hibernian Academy, West was nominated to be one of its original members.

Francis Wheatley (1747–1801) was born in London, the son of a master tailor. He studied at William Shipley's drawing school and the Royal Academy, and won several prizes from the Society of Arts. However, he fell in with extravagant company and was forced to flee his creditors, eloping to Ireland with Elizabeth Gresse, wife of fellow artist John Alexander Gresse. He established himself in Dublin as a portrait-painter, executing, among other works, the best-known interior of the Irish House of Commons.

Leo Whelan (1892–1956) was born in Dublin. He learned drawing and painting at the Metropolitan School of Art under William Orpen, becoming in due course – along with Sean Keating, Margaret Clarke and Patrick Tuohy – one of his most influential pupils in early twentieth-century Irish painting. In 1911, Whelan first showed at the Royal Hibernian Academy. In 1916 he won the Taylor Art Scholarship, and a number of portrait commissions followed. In 1924 Whelan was elected a full member of the

RHA. Throughout the 1930s and 1940s he was much in demand, and continued painting portraits with his usual meticulous clarity.

Maurice Canning Wilks (1910–1984) studied at the Belfast School of Arts. An early exhibitor at the Ulster Academy of Arts, he was elected an associate in 1935. He exhibited widely, including shows at the Royal Hibernian Academy and the Theo Waddington Galleries in Dublin. He also had success abroad, with solo shows in Montreal and Boston during the 1960s.

David Woodlock (1842–1929) was born in Ireland, but is best known as a Liverpool artist. He studied at the Liverpool School of Art and exhibited many works at the Walker Gallery. He was a member of the Liverpool Academy of Arts and a founder member of the Liverpool Sketching Club.

Jack Butler Yeats (1871–1957) was the youngest son of Irish portraitist John Butler Yeats, and brother of the poet W.B. Yeats. His early artworks were romantic depictions of landscapes and figures from the west of Ireland, and he was also a prolific illustrator, producing images for the Dun Emer and Cuala Industries in Dublin as well as work for London-based publishers. After 1920, sympathetic to but not active in the Irish Republican movement, he began to produce more realistic paintings of life in Ireland.

INDEX OF FIRST LINES

ACKNOWLEDGEMENTS (POEMS)

Anon, 'The Mystery' (by permission of Douglas H. Sealy).

Anon, Exile of the Sons of Uisliu *from* 'Táin Bó Cúailnge' (by permission of Thomas Kinsella).

Anon, 'Kilcash' and Egan O'Rahilly, 'Last Lines' (reproduced by permission of PFD on behalf of the Estate of Frank O'Connor; from *Kings, Lords and Commons: an Anthology from the Irish*, © 1959 The Estate of Frank O'Connor).

Anon, 'The Nun of Beare' (reproduced by permission of PFD on behalf of the Estate of Frank O'Connor; from *A Golden Treasury of Irish Poetry*, © 1967 The Estate of Frank O'Connor).

Anon, 'The Day of Wrath' (by permission of Louise Anson).

Anon, 'My Hand Has a Pain from Writing' (© Flann O'Brien; reprinted by permission of A.M. Heath & Co Ltd).

Lord Dunsany, 'The Memory' (from *The Oxford Book of Irish Verse*, Oxford, 1958).

Seumas O'Sullivan, 'The Lamplighter' (by permission of Frances Sommerville; from *Watching the River Flow*, Poetry Ireland, 1999).

Mary Devenport O'Neill, 'Scene-Shifter Death' (from *Ireland's Women: Writings Past and Present*, Gill & Macmillan, 1994)

Padraic Colum, 'She Moved Through the Fair' (by permission of the Estate of Padraic Colum).

Austin Clarke, 'Unmarried Mothers', 'The Planter's Daughter' (by permission of R. Dardis Clarke, 17 Oscar Square, Dublin 8; from *Collected Poems*, Carcanet/The Bridge Press, 2008).

Ewart Milne, 'Diamond Cut Diamond' (from *Diamond Cut Diamond: Selected Poems*, Bodley Head, London, 1953).

Patrick Kavanagh, 'To be Dead', 'Shancoduff' (by permission of the Trustees of the Estate of the later Katherine B. Kavanagh, through the Jonathan Williams Literary Agency; from *Collected Poems*, ed. A. Quinn, Allen Lane, 2004); and *from* 'Lough Derg' (by permission of the Trustees of the Estate of the later Katherine B. Kavanagh, through the Jonathan Williams Literary Agency).

John Hewitt, 'Once Alien Here' (from *No Rebel Word*, Frederick Muller, London, 1948).

Louis MacNeice, 'Dublin' (by permission of the author).

Louis MacNeice *from* 'Autumn Journal' (by permission of the author; from *The Collected Poems of Louis MacNeice*, ed. E.R. Dodds, Faber and Faber, 1966).

Flann O'Brien (Brian O'Nolan), 'The Workman's Friend' (© Flann O'Brien; reprinted by permission of A.M. Heath & Co Ltd).

Leslie Daiken, 'Nostalgie d'Automne' (by permission of Melanie Daiken; from *New Irish Poets*, ed. Devin A. Garrity, Devin-Adair, 1948).

Brendan Behan, 'The Jackeen's Lament for The Blaskets' (from *Watching the River Flow*, Poetry Ireland, 1999).

Maurice James Craig, 'Ballad to a Traditional Refrain' (by permission of the author and the Jonathan Williams Literary Agency).

Robert Greacen, 'The Glorious Twelfth, 12 July 1943' (© Devin-Adair Publishers, Old Greenwich, CT; from *New Irish Poets*, ed. Devin A. Garrity, Devin-Adair, 1948).

Pearse Hutchinson, 'Bright After Dark' (by permission of the author and The Gallery Press, Loughcrew, Oldcastle, County Meath, Ireland; from *Collected Poems*, 2002).

Patrick Galvin, 'The Madwoman of Cork' (by permission of Cork University Press, Youngline Industrial Estate, Pouladuff, Togher, Cork).

Richard Murphy, 'The Reading Lesson' (by permission of the author; © Dennis O'Driscoll).

Thomas Kinsella, 'His Father's Hands' (by permission of the author).

John Montague, 'Like Dolmens Round My Childhood, the Old People' (by permission of the author and The Gallery Press, Loughcrew, Oldcastle, County Meath, Ireland; from *Collected Poems*, 1995).

Seamus Heaney, 'Digging', 'Mid-Term Break' and 'Derry Derry Down' (by permission of the author and Faber & Faber Ltd; from *The Poetry of Seamus Heaney*, 1998).

Michael Longley, 'Ceasefire' (© Michael Longley 2006; c/o LAW, 14 Vernon St, London; from *Selected Poems*, Jonathan Cape, 1994/1998).

Derek Mahon, 'Derry Morning', 'A Disused Shed in Co. Wexford'; 'Antarctica' (by permission of the author and The Gallery Press, Loughcrew, Oldcastle, County Meath, Ireland; from *New Collected Poems*, 2011).

Michael Hartnett, 'Death of an Irishwoman'; 'A Farewell to English' (by permission of the Estate of Michael Hartnett, c/o The Gallery Press, Loughcrew, Oldcastle, County Meath, Ireland; from *Collected Poems*, 2001).

Eiléan Ní Chuilleanáin, 'The Second Voyage' (by permission of the author and The Gallery Press, Loughcrew, Oldcastle, County Meath, Ireland; from *Selected Poems*, 2008).

Macdara Woods, 'Fire and Snow and Carnevale' (by permission of Dedalus Press, 13 Moyclare Road, Baldoyle, Dublin 13).

Eavan Boland, 'Night Feed' (by permission of the author and Carcanet Press, Alliance House, Manchester; from *Night Feed*, 1982).

Paul Durcan, 'Irish Hierarchy Bans Colour Photography' (by permission of the author; from *Life is a Dream: 40 Years Reading Poems 1967–2007*, Harvill Secker, 2009).

Biddy Jenkinson, 'Silence' (by permission of Cork University Press, Youngline Industrial Estate, Pouladuff, Togher, Cork).

Medbh McGuckian, 'The Aphrodisiac' (by permission of the author and The Gallery Press, Loughcrew, Oldcastle, County Meath, Ireland; from *Selected Poems*, 1997).

Paul Muldoon, 'Cuba' (by permission of the author and Faber & Faber Ltd; from *Selected Poems 1968–1983*, 1986).

Nuala Ni Dhomhnaill, 'Blodewedd' (by permission of the author and The Gallery Press, Loughcrew, Oldcastle, County Meath, Ireland; from *Pharaoh's Daughter*, 1990).

Thomas McCarthy, 'The Phenomenology of Stones' (from *The Penguin Book of Contemporary Irish Poetry*, P. Fallon and D. Mahon, eds. Penguin Books, London, 1991).

ACKNOWLEDGEMENTS (PAINTINGS)

The publishers are grateful to the following for their assistance in providing images and information:

Adam's Fine Art Auctioneers and Valuers, 26 St Stephens Green, Dublin 2 www.adams.ie

Crawford Art Gallery, Emmet Place, Cork www.crawfordartgallery.ie

de Veres Art Auctions, 35 Kildare Street, Dublin 2 www.deveresart.com

David Keating for paintings by Sean Keating (pages 115, 149).

Dr Michael Purser for paintings by Sarah Purser (pages 57, 133, 144).

DACS for paintings by Jack B. Yeats (© Estate of Jack B Yeats. All rights reserved, DACS 2011); Markey Robinson (© Estate of Markey Robinson. All rights reserved, DACS 2011); Daniel O'Neill (© Estate of Daniel O'Neill. All rights reserved, DACS 2011); Maurice Wilks (© Estate of Maurice Wilks. All rights reserved, DACS 2011).

Dolans Art House Auction House, 11 Woodquay, Galway, Ireland (page 46).

Dublin City Gallery, The Hugh Lane, Charlemont House, Parnell Square North, Dublin 1 www.hughlane.ie

Felix Rosensteil's Widow and Son Ltd, London on behalf of the Estate of Sir John Lavery for paintings on pages 79, 143, 195.

Limerick City Gallery of Art, Istabraq Hall, City Hall, Merchants Quay, Limerick for permission to use 'The Old Woman' (page 24).

Margaret Early and Gillian Buckley for permission to use 'Cathleen Ni Houlihan (Madonna Irlanda)' (page 197).

Morgan O'Driscoll Fine Art Auctioneers www.morganodriscoll.com

National Museums of Northern Ireland Picture Library, Cultra, Holywood, Co. Down (page 116).

Pierre and Louis le Brocquy for the painting by Louis le Brocquy (page 137).

Sunflower Fine Art Galleries for permission to use 'The Stone Cutter' (page 165) and 'Hog Heaven' (page 188).

Taylor Galleries, 16 Kildare St, Dublin 2 www.taylorgalleries.com

The Estate of David Clarke for permission to use 'High Sky Over The Blaskets' (page 151).

The Estate of William Conor for permission to use 'Coortin' (page 116) and 'Stepping Out Together' (page 117).

The Friends of the National Collections of Ireland for paintings by Evie Hone, © Evie Hone Estate (pages 105, 110). www.fnci.ie

The Kenny Gallery, Liosbán, Tuam Road, Galway (pages 151, 183) www.TheKennyGallery.ie

The National Gallery of Ireland Picture Gallery, Merrion Square West and Clare Street, Dublin 2 www.nationalgallery.ie

The Arts Council of Northern Ireland for permission to use 'Twelfth Parade – North Queen Street'. thestreetgallery.com

Whyte's Fine Art Auctioneers, 38 Molesworth Street, Dublin 2 info@whites.ie

Harry Boyle for permission to use 'St Finbarre' (page 199).

Catriona Kernoff for permission to use 'St Stephen's Green' (page 49); 'A Bird Never Flew on One Wing' (page 53); 'Murphy's Boat-Yard, Ringsend, Dublin' (page 122).

Romelly Leonard for 'Loisceadh Fiaileach, Ruis Eo' (page 77).

Ciarán MacGonigal for permission to use 'The Enraged Woman' (page 158).

Jane O'Malley for permission to use 'Hawk and Quarry in Winter' (page 187).

Annie Robinson for permission to use 'Old Queen's Bridge, Belfast' (page 155).

The publishers are grateful to the following artists or their estates for their assistance and permission to use their work:

Brian Bourke 'Knockalough, Summer' (page 12).

Muriel Brandt 'The Breadline' (page 110).

George Campbell 'Still Life at my Window' (page 146).

Bettie Christie 'Autumn Landscape' (page 141).

Patrick Collins 'Adam and Eve' (page 170).

Barrie Cooke 'Forest' (page 185).

Vicki Crowley 'Bergy Bits, Antarctica' (page 183).

Gerard Dillon 'Old Woman and Washing' (page 171); 'Stunts' (page 91); 'Connemara Lovers' (page 68); 'The End or Not Your Turn Yet' (page 67); and 'Yellow Bungalow' (1916–1971)' (page 135).

Anna Marie Dowdican 'Boat in Reeds' (page 73).

Luke Lawnicki 'Mother' (page 198).

Brian Maguire 'Figure Silenced' (page 102).

Charlotte Mangan 'Show Me the Way to the Lollipop Kids' (page 134).

Joseph McWilliams 'Twelfth Parade – North Queen Street' (page 152) and 'The Orange Parade passing St Patricks Church' (page 153).

Colin Middleton 'August Landscape Boa Island' (page 131) and 'Light of the World: Martyrs of the Vision of St John' (page 179).

Carmel Mooney 'Stone Circle' (page 169).

Mick Mulcahy 'Image from a Remote Silence' (page 45).

Diarmuid O'Ceallachain 'Dripsey Castle' (page 39).

John O'Leary 'Night Odyssey' (page 201).

Daniel O'Neill 'Snow Covered Landscape' (page 193) and 'The Bride' (page 127).

Nano Reid 'Tinkers Gathering Firewood' (page 189).

Robert Ryan 'Deserted Village' (page 52).

Patrick Scott 'Under the Pier' (page 181).

John Vallely (Colin Tilson, photographer) 'Nocturne' (page 71).

Patrick Walshe 'Floating Stones' (page 205).

Leo Whelan 'The Flute Player' (page 75).